SOUTHWEST FLORIDA'S WETLAND WILDERNESS

SOUTHWEST FLORIDA'S

UNIVERSITY PRESS OF FLORIDA

Gainesville   Tallahassee   Tampa   Boca Raton
Pensacola   Orlando   Miami   Jacksonville

WETLAND WILDERNESS

Big Cypress Swamp and the Ten Thousand Islands

Jeff Ripple

Photographs by Clyde Butcher

Paperback edition published 1996 by University Press of Florida
Text copyright 1996 by Jeff Ripple
Photographs copyright 1996 by Clyde Butcher
Foreword copyright 1996 by John H. Fitch
Printed in the United States of America on acid-free paper / All rights reserved
First published 1992 as *Big Cypress Swamp and the Ten Thousand Islands,*
by University of South Carolina Press

06 05 04 03 02 01   7 6 5 4 3 2

LIBRARY OF CONGRESS CATALOGING-IN-PUBLICATION DATA
Ripple, Jeff, 1963–.
Southwest Florida's wetland wilderness: Big Cypress Swamp and the Ten Thousand Islands / by
Jeff Ripple; photographs by Clyde Butcher.
p. cm.
Rev. ed. of: Big Cypress Swamp and the Ten Thousand Islands. 1992.
Includes bibliographical references.
ISBN 0-8130-1454-9 (paper: alk. paper)
I. Natural history—Florida—Big Cypress Swamp. 2. Natural history—Florida—Ten Thousand
Islands. 3. Nature conservation—Florida—Big Cypress Swamp. 4. Nature conservation—Florida
Ten Thousand Islands. 1. Ripple, Jeff, 1963–. Big Cypress Swamp and the Ten Thousand Islands.
II. Title.
QH105.F6R575 1996
508-759'44—dc20   96-33965

The University Press of Florida is the scholarly publishing agency for the State University System
of Florida, comprised of Florida A & M University, Florida Atlantic University, Florida International University, Florida State University, University of Central Florida, University of Florida,
University of North Florida, University of South Florida, and University of West Florida.

University Press of Florida, 15 Northwest 15th Street, Gainesville, FL 32611
http://www.upf.com

*This book is dedicated with gratitude to everyone
involved in the establishment and continued protection
of the Big Cypress National Preserve.*

CONTENTS

FOREWORD

$\mathcal{S}$OUTH FLORIDA is fortunate to have not one but two spectacular subtropical watersheds connecting extensive interior freshwater wetlands with coastal bays and estuaries. Most people have heard of southeast Florida's Everglades, but few are familiar with the Big Cypress Watershed in southwest Florida. This magnificent watershed includes the Big Cypress Swamp, with more than a million acres of interior wetlands, and the Ten Thousand Islands, with one of the world's largest contiguous mangrove forests.

Few regions of the United States have been less understood and less valued than south Florida's watersheds. Their waters have been polluted, their wetlands drained and filled, their natural water flows diverted, and their forests clear-cut. As a result, the Everglades Watershed is now endangered and will not survive without major efforts to curb pollution and restore natural water flow. The prognosis is better for the less-disturbed Big Cypress Watershed, as long as its ecological health and integrity can be sustained.

History has taught us that no major ecosystem, no matter how well protected by land ownership and government regulations, will long endure unless people understand, appreciate, and support its existence. People value only what they understand, and they conserve only what they value. Books like this one contribute much to the public understanding and appreciation of this magnificent subtropical ecosystem and the unique native plants and animals it supports.

To successfully promote conservation, people must be connected with native landscapes and ecosystems on practical, intellectual, emotional, and aesthetic levels. I believe that readers will find these connections in *South-*

west Florida's Wetland Wilderness, with its excellent description of the natural history of the Big Cypress Watershed and its magnificent photographs by Clyde Butcher.

The Big Cypress Watershed must be regarded as a natural trust from the past and a bequest to future generations. All of us have the responsibility to understand and conserve this natural treasure, and *Southwest Florida's Wetland Wilderness* shows us good reasons to do so.

John H. Fitch, President
The Conservancy
Naples, Florida

PREFACE

*T*HE BIG CYPRESS WATERSHED, which includes Big Cypress Swamp and the Ten Thousand Islands, is one of North America's unsung wild places—a beautiful, rugged, subtropical landscape experienced by a relatively few adventurous souls each year. Many who appreciate the unique qualities of this wilderness will argue that it is a place better kept secret. Perhaps, in my quest for solitude and a deeply personal communion with nature, I might ordinarily agree. But I also feel there is an urgent message that must be communicated—one that, if ignored, might allow a terrible tragedy to be visited upon a resource important not only for its natural heritage and spiritually enriching powers, but for its commercial and recreational values as well.

Big Cypress Swamp and the Ten Thousand Islands is a rare and beautiful place. It is a watershed contributing a vital flow of fresh water to southwest Florida's estuaries—nursery grounds for many commercially important fish and shellfish in the Gulf of Mexico. Residents of southwest Florida depend on this watershed as their primary source of fresh water. Although more than one million acres of Big Cypress Swamp have been set aside for preservation by the state and federal governments, as well as by private conservation groups, its natural resources are not safe against waterborne pollutants and the effects of other human activities in surrounding areas. Appropriate safeguards must be instituted and current laws that guarantee protection to the quality of water in the watershed must be stringently enforced to ensure that its pristine character is not sacrificed. The results of decisions we make now regarding how to care for this natural treasure will remain with us for the rest of our lives and will influence the lives of future generations. If we allow Big Cypress Swamp to be defiled, we will lose a precious gift of nature that can never be replaced.

Southwest Florida's Wetland Wilderness: Big Cypress Swamp and the Ten Thousand Islands is a revised, updated, and expanded edition of a book titled *Big Cypress Swamp and the Ten Thousand Islands: Eastern America's Last Great Wilderness*, originally published in 1992 by the University of South Carolina Press. The photographs of Florida artist Clyde Butcher have been added for this edition. The book is an introduction to an ecological treasure matched by few places in the world for diversity of species and variety of ecosystems; many of the species found there are threatened with extinction, and some exist nowhere else in North America. I explore the natural history of the region and chronicle the life stories of many of its fascinating organisms. The final chapter highlights the management responsibilities, recreational opportunities, and interpretive functions provided by parks and preserves within Big Cypress Swamp and the Ten Thousand Islands. A catalog at the end of the book, listing many of the plants and animals in the region, has been added to this edition. I hope that *Southwest Florida's Wetland Wilderness* will both inspire and educate. Perhaps it will even encourage you to do something to protect a wildland close to your heart—wherever that land may be.

ACKNOWLEDGMENTS

Special thanks are in order for the following people: Thom Holloway, who introduced me to the Ten Thousand Islands; Dr. Fred Cichocki and Terry Walker, intrepid field companions on many backcountry outings; Bob Bergen; Pete Brockman (Collier-Seminole State Park); Charles DuToit and Mercedes McCallen; Dr. Jim Snyder, Deborah Jansen, "Buck" Thackerey, and Larry Belles (Big Cypress National Preserve); Peter Dederich; Kevin Fitzgerald; Sandy Dayhoff; Todd Logan; Ed Carlson (National Audubon Society's Corkscrew Swamp Sanctuary); Dr. John Fitch (The Conservancy); and Renée Ripple. Dr. Jim Snyder (Big Cypress National Preserve), Dr. Bill Robertson (Everglades National Park), and Charles DuToit reviewed the manuscript of the original edition.

National parks belong to all of us, but they need our support to continue maintaining the incredible diversity of wildlands, visitor facilities, and educational programs for which they are famous worldwide. A portion of the royalties from this book is being donated to fund the construction and maintenance of boardwalks and associated interpretive materials at Big Cypress National Preserve.

You can help promote a vigorous interpretive program at Big Cypress National Preserve. If you are interested in volunteering your time or expertise, call (941) 695-2000 or write to: Superintendent, Big Cypress National Preserve, HCR 61, Box 110, Ochopee, Florida 33943, for more information.

If you would prefer to make a cash donation, send your check payable to the National Park Service with reference to the Ripple-Butcher Fund to:

Big Cypress National Preserve
Attn: Administration
HCR 61, Box 110
Ochopee, Florida 33943

CHAPTER I

BIG CYPRESS SWAMP

$\mathcal{S}$ IX MILLION YEARS AGO, Big Cypress Swamp bore little resemblance to the varied mosaic of cypress strands, open cypress prairies, freshwater marshes, pinelands, and hardwood hammocks that typify this landscape today. In fact, all of southwest Florida and much of the rest of the state was covered by a warm, shallow sea. Particles of sand, clay, and organic material fell to the bottom of this sea and became marine sediments. Over hundreds of thousands of years and through repeated cycles of rising and falling sea level, these sediments hardened to form limestone. As the sea retreated to near its present level almost 6,000 years ago, southwest Florida's limestone bedrock was exposed, creating a foundation ideal for colonization by hundreds of species of land plants and animals from temperate regions of North America, as well as the tropical West Indies. The Tamiami, Pinecrest, Caloosahatchee, Fort Thompson, and Miami limestone formations lie stacked in uneven layers beneath Big Cypress Swamp, exposed here and there as low ridges and outcrops in the pinelands and hardwood hammocks. This porous limestone is also visible through a thin veneer of sawgrass and dwarf cypress in shallow freshwater marshes and wet prairies. Other times the rock may show itself along the crumbling edges of solution holes.

The terrain throughout much of Big Cypress Swamp appears flat, but subtle variations in the bedrock result in different land forms, hydrological patterns, soil types, and plant communities. A matter of a few inches of elevation may determine whether a cypress strand or a pine forest covers a stretch of bedrock. Rainwater, the probing roots of trees and vegetation, and chemical reactions between decaying organic matter and the limestone in turn exert their influence on the bedrock and reshape the very foundation of the swamp itself.

The subtropical influence of southwest Florida's climate is clearly evident by its well-defined rainy and dry seasons—almost 80 percent of the region's fifty-five or more inches of annual rainfall occurs from May through October. Late afternoon thunderstorms during the rainy season roll in from the Gulf of Mexico or spend the day building themselves into billowing thunderheads that suddenly erupt with lightning, thunder, and torrents of rain. Showers are much less frequent during the dry season, November through April; most winter rain accompanies cold fronts that move down through the state from the northern United States. As a result of the seasonal rainfall pattern, water rises to flood much of Big Cypress Swamp during the rainy season. The water gradually recedes through the winter and sometimes dries up altogether by late spring. Throughout the evolution of Big Cypress Swamp, those plants and animals that have been able to adapt to this seasonal cycle of flood and drought survive, while those that cannot gradually disappear.

CYPRESS FORESTS

Although Big Cypress Swamp contains several distinct plant communities, it is the cypress forests that dominate the landscape. Big Cypress Swamp is named not for the size of its cypress, but rather for the impressive amount of territory covered by them. Geologists believe that cypress have been present in southwest Florida for just over five thousand years—a relatively short period given the earth's more than four-billion-year history.

Many cypress and mixed swamp forests in Big Cypress form long, winding "strands" or "sloughs" that follow shallow north to southwest depressions in the bedrock. Fakahatchee, Deep Lake, East Hinson, Gator Hook, and Roberts Lake are among the largest strands, creating dense green fingers that push their way through the marshes, prairies, and scattered open pine forests. The popular theory explaining the origin of these strands points to ancient dunes, offshore bars, or sand spits that solidified and then collapsed due to erosion and the gradual dissolution of the limestone by pooling rainwater and acids from decaying organic material. This same process created thousands of circular or egg-shaped depressions in the central and eastern portions of Big Cypress, from which cypress domes or "heads" pop up like little islands surrounded by a sea of cordgrass and sawgrass. In some cases, the center of a depression is too deep for cypress or other trees to grow, thereby creating an open pool. The pool gives the dome a "doughnut-hole" appearance from the air. Alligators often move into a cypress dome and keep these holes clear of debris and vegetation, providing permanent homes for themselves and important water sources for other wildlife during the dry season.

The wet organic soil found in most cypress forests provides poor anchoring for large trees like cypress. However, cypress do have several ways to protect themselves against occasional high winds. Their small, feathery needles offer little resistance to wind, and their branches are relatively short compared to the massive trunks. Extremely high winds, such as those that occur during hurricanes, can sever the tops of large cypress, but the trees remain standing and will eventually grow new crowns.

Two species of cypress are found in Big Cypress Swamp—bald cypress and pond cypress. They are deciduous conifers (related to the redwoods of California) that drop their needles in November and burst forth with new growth by late February or March. Cypress are wholly dependent on fluctuating water levels to compete with faster-growing hardwoods for the limited resources available beneath the canopy. Where logging was most intensive or fire has swept through and killed much of the cypress, the forests have become a mixed swamp where cypress share the upper reaches of the canopy with other hardwoods.

Bald cypress and pond cypress generally differ in branch structure, foliage, bark, and seedlings. A pond cypress can usually be distinguished from bald cypress by its needles, which are scale-like and point upward, unlike those of the bald cypress, which are feather-like and lie flat on the plane of the branches. Mature bald and pond cypress both develop characteristic buttresses of various sizes and shapes, in addition to the unusual "knees" that many botanists believe may help support the trees and aerate the root systems. Pond cypress survive better than bald cypress in areas with less water flow and fewer nutrients, and as a result they form the perimeter of smaller trees that surrounds cypress strands and heads. Dwarf cypress, often called hatrack cypress or scrub cypress, are stunted forms of pond cypress that eke out their existence on the bedrock and thin soil of many prairies in Big Cypress. These trees are frequently hundreds of years old, yet may stand just over six feet tall and measure only twenty inches in diameter.

Cypress seedlings rely on a complex set of circumstances in order to successfully germinate and mature. Male and female cones appear on the same tree and develop from December through March, which coincides with southwest Florida's dry season and the subsequent lowering of water levels throughout Big Cypress Swamp. Ideally, when a cypress seed falls, there will be enough water so that the seed can remain immersed anywhere from one to three months, thereby allowing water to penetrate its thick outer coating. Cypress seeds can float and remain alive when submerged for up to a year; however, they cannot germinate underwater and so must eventually settle into moist soil. After a seedling has poked its way up through the peat and soggy mat of decaying leaves and needles, it must grow quickly to prevent being flooded when water levels rise during the rainy season. In deeper sloughs where the trees ultimately reach their greatest heights, extended dry spells must occur if the seedlings are to survive. Cypress seedlings drown if they are flooded for long periods, but will wilt if the peat soil becomes too dry. However, once cypress mature, they can survive both extended droughts and flooding, making them among the hardiest trees in the swamp.

Well-established cypress communities develop characteristic dome-shaped profiles that on moonlit nights resemble dark hills looming up from the surrounding prairies. Within a cypress dome, older, larger trees inhabit the innermost reaches, thereby creating the peak of the dome. This is because peat layers are thicker in the forest's interior and remain damp, even during severe droughts. The saturated peat provides a moist microclimate that boosts humidity within the forest and helps shelter the large trees from fire. Moving outward from the center of the dome, the trees are typically younger and smaller and form the cypress dome's downward slopes. Peat layers tend to thin toward the edges of the dome, meaning that cypress on the perimeter have less access to nutrients and will therefore be less likely to grow as tall as trees in the interior. Cypress on the perimeter of domes and large strands are also more susceptible to fires that periodically sweep through surrounding prairies and pinelands, further limiting their growth and chances of surviving to an old age.

Vegetation in Cypress Forests

Hundreds of other plant species inhabit cypress forests in addition to cypress. Many of these are hardwoods that compete with cypress (especially seedlings) for light, space, and nutrients beneath the sheltering canopy of large trees. These "subcanopy" hardwoods include red maple, swamp bay, pop ash, and pond apple. When large cypress are logged or otherwise removed, subcanopy hardwoods replace them as the dominant trees and the forest is then considered a mixed swamp forest. Understory plants include ferns, buttonbush, cocoplum, and aquatic species, such as bladderworts and water lilies. Bromeliads and orchids adorn the trunks and branches of many trees, especially the larger cypress and pond apples. The bright red bracts on which the small purple flowers of stiff-leaved wild pine are borne brighten cypress forests in late January through March. Orchids bloom throughout the year.

Bromeliads and orchids common to cypress forests within Big Cypress Swamp are predominantly epiphytes—nonparasitic plants that depend on their host trees for little more than a secure perch. Some epiphytes filter nutrients from dust or leaf debris trapped in their leaves and roots, while others catch minerals in rainwater that washes down from the leaves and bark of their host tree. Thirteen species of bromeliads have been identified in the Fakahatchee Strand, including the strap-leaved air plant, a species found nowhere else in North America. Many large bromeliads collect several quarts of water in the cup-like bases of their leaves. These leafy basins also provide perfect homes for a multitude of small frogs, insects, and lizards.

Most orchids prefer densely vegetated areas with high humidity, and in Big Cypress Swamp they are found mainly on large pond apples, pop ash, and cypress near the deeper sloughs. Fakahatchee Strand harbors several tropical orchids that occur nowhere else in the United States, including the leafless orchid, hidden orchid, and dwarf epidendrum. Cowhorn orchids and rare ghost orchids have been found in Fakahatchee Strand, although they also occur in other areas of southern Florida and in the West Indies. Ionopsis, clamshell orchids, and night-blooming epidendrum are common epiphytes throughout the Caribbean, Central America, and northern South America, but reach the northernmost limits of their range in the frost-free hammocks and mixed swamp forests of Big Cypress.

Other epiphytic plants besides bromeliads and orchids are found in Big Cypress Swamp as well. Several species of ferns lead an epiphytic existence attached to living trees, rotting logs, and even the limestone walls of solution holes. Of these ferns, the resurrection fern is among the most unusual. It cannot store water and if several days pass without rain, it curls up and turns brown, appearing dead until the next rain brings it back to life.

Wildlife in Cypress Forests

Cypress and mixed swamp environments are used extensively by many birds and animals, including migrating warblers and other songbirds, wading birds, red-shouldered hawks, swallow-tailed kites, turkeys, barred and great horned owls, alligators, white-tailed deer, river otters, black bears, and some of the few remaining Florida panthers. As habitat, they are critical to the survival of several species of frogs, turtles, and snakes; wood ducks; great crested flycatchers; and gray and Big Cypress (mangrove) fox squirrels.

One endangered species that depends heavily on cypress forests for nesting is the wood stork. In the 1930s, Florida's nesting population of wood storks was believed to be more than 75,000 birds, more than 20,000 of which nested in Big Cypress Swamp. However, during the last sixty years, the entire wood stork population has dwindled to less than 10 percent of their original numbers. The National Audubon Society's Corkscrew Swamp Sanctuary in the northwest corner of Big Cypress Swamp is one of the few remaining places where the birds still nest in southern Florida, and there are often intervals of several years between successful breeding seasons.

The major cause of the stork's dramatic decline appears to be inadequate reproduction, a problem stemming from changes in the timing and rate that water disappears from Big Cypress Swamp during the dry season. Wood storks are specialized feeders that require shallow water with concentrated populations of fish, crayfish, tadpoles, and frogs. Unlike herons and egrets, which hunt by patiently waiting for prey and then spearing it with their sharp beaks, wood storks are "grope" or "tactile" feeders, which means that they capture food by touch. This is an advantage when the water is murky and their small prey cannot be seen from the surface. A wood stork's beak is extremely sensitive, and when an unfortunate killifish or other morsel bumps the searching beak, it is snapped up in less than one-fortieth of a second. This reaction is one of the fastest known in nature. Unfortunately, if the water is too deep and the fish are widely dispersed, the stork must work much harder to catch the three-and-a-half pounds of fish it needs each day to feed itself and nestlings. Biologists estimate that a single family of wood storks can gulp down more than 440 pounds of food each breeding season.

Historically, wood storks timed their breeding cycle to coincide with the seasonal dry-down as rains tapered off in Big Cypress toward the end of October. As water levels dropped, fish and other small creatures were trapped in thousands of shallow pools as the surrounding marshes dried up. This drying process began first in ponds located in upland areas and progressed to lower-lying ponds, prairies, and sloughs as the dry season continued. The gradual dry-down ensured that wood storks and other wading birds would have a continuous supply of concentrated food throughout the breeding season. Wood storks must form colonies and begin nesting between November and January to successfully raise their young before the rains begin in June. If water levels are unusually high or low during the winter, the adult birds will be unable to find enough food to sustain themselves and their chicks, even though they are capable of flying on long trips of up to 100 miles in search of good feeding areas. In this event, nests are usually abandoned and the half-grown chicks left to starve. Fresh water throughout much of southern Florida is managed primarily for human use, meaning that thousands of acres of wetlands are either too wet or too dry at the height of the birds' breeding season. Without a significant change in water management policies, the wood stork's future will be one of continued decline.

Logging the Cypress Forests

Much of the cypress in Big Cypress Swamp was cut during extensive lumbering operations that reached their peak in the 1930s and 1940s. Logging was concentrated in large, heavily forested strands, such as Fakahatchee, Deep Lake, Roberts Lake, and Gator Hook. These strands were essentially cleared of old-growth cypress that may have been several hundred years old and exceeded heights of 130 feet. The huge trees were often girdled with an axe a couple of months before they were cut so that they would die and dry out. Dry trees weighed considerably less than trees cut fresh and thus were easier to handle when they were finally felled and dragged to the mills by mules, oxen, small bulldozers, and even trains. Smaller cypress were sometimes taken as well, which further depleted the strands. Any cypress eight inches in diameter at its thinnest point and at least thirty feet high was targeted by the sawyers. The only large cypress that escaped logging were trees located too far from a tram system to be economically feasible for harvest. In the Fakahatchee Strand, very few old-growth cypress were spared, and most of those were hollow trees that were not worth cutting. It was from these few isolated old trees and young cypress too small to cut that today's cypress forests were born. Now, the only signs of past logging operations are old stumps, survey markers, and many miles of logging tramroads in the Fakahatchee. Most of the tramroads are covered by a dense growth of palms, hardwoods, ferns, and other vegetation.

Fortunately for the new generation of cypress and mixed swamp forests, most of Big Cypress Swamp is protected from the widespread lumbering that decimated the old-growth cypress of the past. Time, environmentally sensitive water management, and continued preservation will allow the young forests to grow and nourish a tapestry of life forms nearly as amazing as that which greeted the first explorers to Big Cypress.

Marshes and prairies in Big Cypress Swamp are generally grouped under four broad categories: dry prairies, wet prairies, freshwater marshes, and saltwater marshes. There are rarely abrupt transitions between these ecosystems, and they frequently overlap. In this flat land where differences in elevation are measured in inches, freshwater marshes and wet prairies typically occupy middle ground between high pineland areas and low-lying cypress strands and domes. Dry prairies develop on dry, open areas between pineland communities, while saltwater marshes form a narrow band along the southern edge of Big Cypress Swamp between the freshwater marshes to the north and the broad mangrove forest that reaches south to the sinuous channels and shallow bays of the Ten Thousand Islands.

Dry Prairies

Dry prairies cover an extremely small portion of Big Cypress Swamp. Plants that typically dominate dry prairies include low, scrubby saw palmettos, wire grass, and a mix of other grasses. Dry prairies are rarely flooded and may burn as often as once a year. Fire recycles nutrients and kills hardwoods that could eventually overgrow the prairie if left unchecked by the flames. The browns and greens of the dry prairies are brightened by wildflowers such as goldenrod, milkworts, bachelor's buttons, and sabatia, as well as by several species of butterflies.

Wet Prairies

Wet prairies, as their name implies, remain flooded or at least spongy wet for two to five months out of the year. Most of these prairies are found on mineral soils overlying the limestone bedrock. Cordgrass and sawgrass are two of the most common components of the wet prairies, with a healthy mix of other grasses, sedges, and rushes adding to the prairie's diversity. Although wildflowers provide smatterings of color in the wet prairies year round, during spring and summer the color spreads to form a carpet of yellows, pinks, purples, whites, and reds mixed among the bright green of new grasses. Marsh pinks, grass pinks, sabatia, false foxglove, coreopsis, goldenrod, swamp milkweed, swamp lilies, and bachelor's buttons are only a few members of the vast array of wildflowers found in the wet prairies from March through October.

Larger animals such as deer, bobcats, and raccoons often venture onto the wet prairies, but it is the tiny creatures that form the bulk of the animal population. Green tree frogs, little grass frogs, toothpick and longhorned grasshoppers, several species of orb weaver spiders, and crab spiders live among the blades of grass and wildflower petals. Green anoles sit in wait for ants on the scattered cypress that grow in many wet prairies. Frequently called "chameleons" for their ability to change from bright green to various shades of brown, these four- to six-inch lizards depend more on their camouflage than on swift escape as a defense against predators.

During the summer and well into fall, a wet prairie may be covered by as much as six inches of water. Beneath the water's surface, a teeming population of snails, freshwater shrimp, killifish, mosquito fish, and aquatic insects wriggle among the submerged bases of the grasses and sedges. As rains taper off and water levels in the wet prairie drop, these creatures migrate to deeper marshes and sloughs, or burrow under the mud to wait until the prairies are inundated once again. Unfortunately, a consequence of the falling water levels is a decrease in dissolved oxygen. As long as the animals do not exhaust the oxygen available in their pool, they will survive. Wading birds follow the line of receding water and converge on the shallow pools, feeding voraciously on the concentrated fish. This not only provides a critical source of food for the wading birds and their nestlings, but also increases the chance that the remaining aquatic animals in the pools will survive to repopulate surrounding areas when the rains return.

Periphyton is a major component of the aquatic vegetation found in wet prairies. This slimy, greenish mat is made up of blue-green and green algae that grow on bare substrates or on other vegetation, forming a blanket of life that covers the bottom. These algae are eaten by several species of flies, snails, zooplankton, and fish, thereby establishing themselves as fundamental links in the food chain. The blue-green algae also contribute large amounts of calcium carbonate, which forms the calcitic mud, or marl, that is a common substrate throughout Big Cypress Swamp. During the dry season, the periphyton dries out to form stiff, greyish-white strands that drape from the grasses and coat the cracked mud surface of the wet prairie.

Freshwater Marshes

Freshwater marshes, many of which may be hard to distinguish from wet prairies, develop in areas typically flooded anywhere from six to nine months out of the year. Some marshes may border alligator holes or permanent ponds and only rarely dry out. Marsh communities may also form in shallower areas of canals, such as sites that have been partially filled in by the National Park Service along the Turner River Canal. During the dry season, deer use these areas for water and raccoons hunt for food along the shoreline, while river otters raise their young in dens along the bank and fish the deeper, open pools. Small flocks of wood storks, white ibis, great egrets, and snowy egrets feed among the cattails. When water levels are ideal and the fishing is good, great blue herons stake out areas about 200 feet apart, although they share them with smaller waders like little blue herons, tricolored herons, green herons, and limpkins. Anhingas and common moorhens are perennial residents, while black-crowned night herons, yellow-crowned night herons, and least bitterns are somewhat more rare.

Freshwater marshes are often dominated by one or two plant species that lend their names to the common description of the community, such as sawgrass/cordgrass marsh, cattail marsh, or "flag" marsh. Flag marshes, which get their name from the flag-like leaves of species such as arrowroot, fireflag, and pickerelweed, are frequently found in small depressions within cypress strands and wet prairies. Sawgrass/cordgrass marshes are found throughout much of Big Cypress Swamp and often provide the grassy understory of dwarf cypress forests. Extensive cattail marshes, such as those covering portions of the Arthur R. Marshall Loxahatchee National Wildlife Refuge in the northeastern Everglades, are almost nonexistent in Big Cypress Swamp, although there is a large cattail marsh dotted with cabbage palm heads on the north side of the Tamiami Trail (U.S. 41) near the western edge of Big Cypress National Preserve. This marsh marks a transition zone between wet prairies to the north of the Tamiami Trail and a fringe of saltwater marshes to the south. Some ecologists believe that the proliferation of cattails is caused by the damming effect of the Tamiami Trail and the resulting accumulation of nutrients as water flows from north to south toward the estuaries of the Ten Thousand Islands.

Many freshwater marshes in Big Cypress Swamp are rather small and occur as clusters of sawgrass, cattails, and flags growing within wet prairie communities. A marsh of this nature typically retains water long after the surrounding prairie has dried up, providing a haven for frogs, snails, crayfish, and other creatures that depend on the constant supply of fresh water to survive. Flags and cattails in the marsh tower over the knee-high cordgrass of the wet prairie. Throughout the night, the marsh makes itself heard as hundreds of frogs bark out their calls from the tall vegetation in a cacophony of peeps, croaks, grunts, whistles, and other bizarre noises.

The health of many freshwater marshes depends largely on maintenance by alligators. Alligators keep areas of open water in the marshes clear and deep by preventing a buildup of sediments and vegetation. Their paths help flood marshes during the rainy season. Alligator holes and dens may be the last places to hold water at the height of the dry season, providing a critical refuge for aquatic creatures.

Alligators are "cold-blooded," a relatively imprecise term used to describe reptiles, amphibians, and other creatures that lack sophisticated internal mechanisms for maintaining a constant internal body temperature. As a result, their body temperature fluctuates with that of their surroundings. Alligators haul themselves out on logs and muddy banks to bask in the sun and warm up. When their body temperature climbs too high, they slip into the water to cool off. Sometimes, basking with only part of the body exposed is the key to maintaining a body temperature that requires little movement by the animal for most of the day.

Alligators swim by folding their legs along their body and sweeping their tail from side to side. Although they appear sluggish on land, they are capable of moving with amazing speed and can outrun a person over a short distance.

Almost anything that does not walk, swim, fly, crawl, or wriggle out of the way quick enough is a potential meal for an alligator. Prey is captured by stalking, by lying motionless on the bottom, or by hiding in vegetation at the water's surface with only eyes and nostrils exposed. An alligator generally grabs its victim with the side of its jaw rather than head on, and food is swallowed by raising the head and gulping. Small prey, such as a turtle, is crushed and swallowed whole, while larger prey is dragged under and then torn apart and swallowed. Hatchling alligators feast on insects, tiny fish, crabs, crayfish, frogs, snails, and similar morsels. The menu for larger alligators includes fish, turtles, mammals, snakes, crabs, crayfish, birds, insects, and even other alligators. Humans are not on the list of preferred food groups, although alligators may become quite aggressive if they are fed and thereby grow accustomed to associating people with an easy meal. In other words, feeding alligators is dangerous—not to mention illegal—so don't do it.

Alligators court in May, at the beginning of the rainy season. Both male and female alligators advertise their presence and social position by bellowing. To bellow, an alligator arches its head and tail, breathes in, and vibrates air in the throat. The roaring of the males is generally deeper than that of females, and individual alligators can recognize each other by their bellows. Alligators bellow throughout the year, but this activity is more frequent during courtship.

Courting alligators swim and sun together for several days. On land, a male alligator sometimes strokes the female with his front foot. In the water, they often float with their heads together, sometimes nose to nose or with their necks touching. Other romantic activity involves circling, bubble blowing, and spewing water from the nostrils. These quiet moments may be interrupted by bouts of violent thrashing as the couples test their strength by trying to press each other underwater.

Late June to early July finds female alligators busy selecting nest sites and beginning construction of their large nest mounds. Alligator nests are situated at the edges of tree islands or surrounded by open marsh. Nest material, such as sawgrass, cattails, and leaves, is uprooted and piled with mud into a mound high enough to remain above the summer high-water level. The female digs a hole near the top and deposits approximately forty leathery eggs. The eggs incubate for several weeks, warmed by the sun and the decaying vegetation in the nest. The sex of the hatchling alligators is determined by the temperature of the eggs during the first three weeks. It is usually warmest at the top of the nest because of heat from the sun, so most of these eggs develop into males. Eggs toward the bottom of the nest generally remain cooler, and they produce more females.

Throughout the incubation period, female alligators jealously guard their nests against all intruders. Raccoons are common nest marauders and will decimate unguarded nests. Red-bellied turtles sometimes trespass on unwatched alligator nests as well, but for a different reason. A female red-belly scrapes away some of the top material of the nest and lays her clutch of eggs with the alligator's. She then departs, leaving her eggs to be unknowingly watched over by the female alligator.

Baby alligators emit a hiccup-like grunt when they are ready to emerge from the nest. Although they are capable of escaping the nest without assistance, their calls attract their mother, who scrapes away the top portion of the nest with alternating strokes of her front feet, allowing her offspring to tumble into the water. She may also help some eggs hatch by taking them into her mouth, gently cracking them, and allowing the babies to wriggle out between her teeth. Upon entering the water, the young alligators immediately begin feeding on minnows, water beetles, and other small creatures they encounter near the nest. Young alligators can survive on their own, but their chances of escaping predators such as wading birds, large fish, otters, and other alligators are better when they stay together as a group under the watchful eyes of their mother. The group—called a pod—may stay together for only a few days or for as long as several months. A pod of young alligators often finds a mother alligator's head and back the perfect platform for basking. The mother keeps her pod together with low "umph-umph-umph" sounds.

Salt Marshes

Salt marshes cover only a small portion of Big Cypress Swamp and are regarded by some ecologists as an ecotone between the mangroves and the freshwater wetlands. In fact, in some areas patches of salt-marsh plants grow interspersed with freshwater species like sawgrass, cattails, and spikerush. Typical salt-marsh plant species include several cordgrasses, glasswort and saltwort, and Christmas berry. Wading birds such as great white herons, great egrets, glossy and white ibises, and little blue herons can sometimes be seen feeding in the marshes, while marsh hawks swoop low in search of cotton rats and marsh rabbits. Bobcats hunt for rats and rabbits in the grasses as well. Black bears are spotted on rare occasions ambling across the salt marshes on their way to the thicker growth of hardwood hammocks.

The Influence of Water and Fire

Periodic fires and the seasonal fluctuations in water levels work hand in hand with various other factors to fashion the mosaic of different marsh and prairie communities in Big Cypress Swamp. The composition of soils, depth of peat deposits, frost, and underlying geology all contribute to the equation determining which plant and animal species will dominate a community. However, the influences of water and fire are paramount, and they play the greatest role in shaping the face of these grassy landscapes.

As the rainy season commences, water rises to flood the marshes and wet prairies. Hydrologists refer to the amount of time that water covers a plant community as its hydroperiod. The length of the hydroperiod can be important in determining which plants will be present in a community, and fluctuations in water levels are critical to the life cycles of several species. For example, many plants cannot germinate under water and require a dry period in order to sprout and become established. The timing and length of the dry season, combined with the variety of seeds imbedded in the soil, determine which plants will gain a foothold in a particular wet prairie or marsh community. Once they have become established, perennial species such as sawgrass can propagate vegetatively and do not rely on a seed base to spread. As long as they are able to survive under the conditions dictated by other environmental conditions, such as fire and soil type, their continued presence in the plant community is ensured.

Fire plays its part in shaping the ecology of the wet prairies and marshes of Big Cypress Swamp by limiting the invasion of woody plants and influencing the composition of herbaceous plants in these communities. Natural fires are caused by lightning strikes in late spring or early summer when water levels are at their lowest point. In most cases, these fires consume surface vegetation, but do not burn through the thin soil and peat to the limestone bedrock. The fires also prune back small hardwoods, such as bays and wax myrtle, that invade the prairies and marshes if there is a long interval between fires. Without periodic fires, hardwoods would eventually dominate the herbaceous plants, and the area would evolve into either a hardwood hammock or cypress swamp, depending on the length of the hydroperiod.

When a fire burns through an area, it releases nutrients back into the soil and creates an explosion of vegetative growth. In fact, within a few days after a fire, shoots of green can be seen sprouting through the ashes of the old prairie or marsh. This remarkable revitalization increases the diversity of vegetation by enabling the survival of annual plants and low-growing species that would otherwise be completely shut out by sawgrass, cordgrass, and other dominant prairie species. Burning also provides fresh, nutrient-rich plant growth that is an important food source for wildlife.

HARDWOOD HAMMOCKS

Hardwood hammocks, or hardwood tree islands as they are sometimes called, are scattered over marshes and open cypress prairies throughout southern Florida. These forest systems represent what ecologists consider to be the pinnacle of forest development in this region. Fire can be devastating to hammocks, and most hammocks are protected by a moat of deeper water on all sides or by thick vegetation capable of trapping humidity and soil moisture. Solution holes created as a result of the dissolution of limestone by organic material pock the interiors of many hammocks, raising the humidity and providing a source of water for hammock wildlife. A dense, closed canopy of temperate and tropical hardwoods also traps moisture and moderates temperatures within hammocks, in effect creating a "microclimate" that helps protect fragile tropical species from fire and frost damage. Hammocks are generally a few degrees cooler than the surrounding landscape on hot days and are warmer during rare cold snaps.

Temperate and Tropical Hammocks

Hardwood hammocks develop on limestone outcrops or ridges that raise them slightly above the surrounding terrain. Hammocks in the northern reaches of the swamp are made up of a predominantly temperate assortment of trees, including laurel oak, live oak, cabbage palm, and red maple. Warmer temperatures and closer proximity to the coast have given hardwood hammocks in the Pinecrest region and southern areas of the swamp a more tropical nature. These hammocks, appropriately dubbed "tropical hardwood hammocks," are dominated by broad-leaved tropical trees and shrubs with correspondingly exotic names, such as gumbo limbo, pigeon plum, Jamaica dogwood, mastic, wild tamarind, poisonwood, satin leaf, and cocoplum. Majestic Florida royal palms are also common in some hammocks. Tropical hardwood hammocks that develop close to the coast, such as Royal Palm Hammock at Collier-Seminole State Park, may be bordered by saltwater marshes and mangrove forest and boast an even richer assortment of tropical plants. Although hammocks are perched on higher ground than surrounding plant communities, they sometimes flood during extremely high tides or after heavy rains. Periodic flooding in the hammocks is important to tropical species as a means to establish themselves in new territory. Ninety percent of the tropical species that have colonized hardwood hammocks in Big Cypress Swamp originated from such locales as the West Indies and the Yucatán peninsula, carried as seeds by storms and birds.

Vegetation in Tropical Hardwood Hammocks

Tropical hardwood hammocks exude lushness. Living green things are literally stacked on top of each other in their competition for limited light and growing space. Ferns carpet the forest floor, lichens and mosses permeate rotting logs and the bark of living trees, and epiphytic bromeliads and orchids commandeer every square inch of available space along the heavy, spreading lower branches of rough-barked trees. One tropical tree, the strangler fig, takes a rather insidious shortcut in its attempt to gain a foothold in the hammock. Although it can develop free-standing, the strangler fig frequently germinates from a seed dropped by a bird into the upper branches of a large tree. As the seedling grows, it sends down aerial root tendrils that wrap around its host tree on their descent to the hammock floor. The young strangler's grip tightens around the host as its roots thicken, and its branches begin to reach upward to dominate its area of the canopy, crowding out other trees. Even though a strangler fig is not parasitic, the host eventually succumbs when it can no longer compete with the strangler for light and space. Devil's claw, a large, woody tropical vine, also uses a host tree to get a start in life. This vine's hooked thorns help it to literally claw its way from the hammock floor into the canopy. It too may one day ungraciously outcompete its host for light in the crowded upper reaches of the canopy.

Wildlife in Tropical Hardwood Hammocks

The relatively high ground, cover, and abundant food provided by hardwood hammocks make them choice habitat for creatures that prefer less soggy quarters than other areas of Big Cypress Swamp can offer. Gray squirrels and short-tailed shrews are two small mammals that rely heavily on hardwood hammocks for permanent homes, while black bears, white-tailed deer, and Florida panthers are members of the bed and breakfast club, requiring little more from a hammock than a dry place to feed and rest. Several reptiles prowl the hammock floor, including the southeastern five-lined skink, brown anole (an "exotic" or non-native species), green anole, black racer, Florida brown snake, Everglades and yellow rat snakes, southern ringneck snake, and Florida box turtle. However, the invertebrates hold top honors for beauty in the hammocks. Striking orange and black-striped ruddy daggerwing butterflies and equally exquisite black-and-yellow zebra butterflies flit among the undergrowth, while golden orb weavers and crab-like spiny orb weavers spin their sticky, filmy webs to snare mosquitoes and flies.

Perhaps the most beautiful inhabitants of the tropical hardwood hammocks are *Liguus* tree snails. *Liguus* (which means banded) tree snails are the living jewels of the hammocks, bedecked in delicately hued whorls of emerald green, brown, orange, yellow, and pink. Southern Florida's *Liguus* (or "lig") population is believed to have tropical origins and may have descended from snails that floated over on logs from Cuba or Hispaniola, where similar species can still be found today. From this original group of tropical immigrants, more than fifty distinctive color forms have developed in the relative isolation of single hammocks or small groups of hammocks in Big Cypress Swamp, the Everglades, the Ten Thousand Islands, and the Florida Keys.

Ligs are usually found on smooth-barked trees such as wild tamarind, pigeon plum, and Jamaica dogwood. A lig scrapes the bark of these trees for lichens and algae, using a rasp-like tongue called a radula and leaving a cleaned surface and a trail of slime in its wake. It glides along the tree bark by contracting its large foot over a thin layer of mucus secreted from special glands in the sole of the foot. During its feeding forays up and down a tree, a lig may browse over about twenty-five feet of bark a day. Its head, located on the front of the foot, has two pairs of retractable tentacles. At the tip of each of the longer pair of tentacles is a primitive eye, with which the snail may be able to distinguish close objects, as well as the difference between light and dark. The smaller tentacles are sensing organs, which the snail uses to feel its way about its surroundings.

Ligs are most active during the warm, wet summer months, especially after a rain. They are sensitive to cold, and occasional hard freezes kill many snails in less-sheltered areas of the hammocks. To survive southern Florida's dry season, a lig estivates by fastening itself securely to a branch with mucus, which hardens into a weather-tight seal that protects it from drying out. If it is pried off its branch and the mucus seal is broken, the snail will probably die.

Liguus tree snails begin to seek mates in late summer. They are hermaphroditic, which means that each snail has both male and female sex organs. Courtship and mating may take up to two days, after which time each snail glides down to the base of the tree to carve out a hole in the moist leaf litter and lay fifteen to fifty pea-sized eggs. The snail then covers the nest and crawls back up the tree. The eggs lie tucked away in their nests through the winter until warm spring rains trigger the baby snails, or "buttons," to emerge and ascend the tree to begin foraging. Each button will add two or three whorls to its shell during its first year, one or two whorls its second year, and then perhaps one whorl each year after that until it is between two and three inches long. Most shells spiral to the right as they grow, but occasionally "lefties" are found.

Opossums, raccoons, hermit crabs, and rats dine on ligs when they can catch them, but the forces that caused the extinction of several varieties of these beautiful snails were collectors and habitat destruction. In the early part of the century, snail collectors would capture rare color forms of *Liguus* from hammocks in isolated areas of the Everglades and Big Cypress Swamp and then burn the hammocks. This increased the value of their shells because it became more difficult for other collectors to find the varieties endemic to those hammocks. Today, *Liguus* tree snails are protected by state law.

PINELANDS

High ground in Big Cypress Swamp is not the sole domain of hardwood hammocks. Much of the swamp's upland areas are covered by open subtropical pine forests comprised of south Florida slash pine, cabbage palm, saw palmetto, and scattered hardwood shrubs and trees. Saw palmetto and mixed grasses are the two dominant types of understory, although an interesting blend of other temperate and West Indian plant species occur in pineland understories as well. More than 300 species of plants are found in the saw palmetto/pine communities, and no fewer than 360 species grow in the mixed grass/pine areas. The staggering variety of species in the pinelands make these among the most diverse plant communities in southern Florida.

Pinelands develop on land that is several inches to a few feet above that of surrounding prairies and cypress, which means they occupy some of the driest ground in Big Cypress Swamp. Some pinelands are found on out-crops of exposed Tamiami limestone. However, this doesn't mean that they escape flooding; in fact, many pineland communities, especially those in the eastern region of Big Cypress Swamp, are frequently flooded. The pinelands with a mixed grass understory are usually flooded for longer peri-ods throughout the year than are the saw palmetto/pine forests.

The Role of Fire in Pineland Communities

All pinelands depend on fire to maintain their vigor and diversity, and all pineland species have adapted to it in one way or another. South Florida slash pine, the dominant pineland tree in Big Cypress, is covered by a thick, corky, outer bark that protects the fragile inner plant material from heat and flames, while its long needles shield its vulnerable apical buds. Another com-mon pineland plant, the saw palmetto, survives fires by protecting its vul-nerable living tissues within a recessed bud hidden under scaly leaf bases. Openings created in a pine forest understory after a fire allow new pine seed-lings to become established due to reduced vegetative litter, additional nu-trients in the soil, and more exposure to sunlight.

Another significant effect of fire is that it synchronizes the reproductive activity of grasses and wildflowers. In unburned pinelands, some species of grasses and wildflowers bloom sporadically; many don't flower at all. How-ever, in the flowering season after a fire, a pineland understory may be burst-ing with color as every plant of a particular species flowers simultaneously. Because several species share the same flowering season, the new growth in a pineland can be both prolific and beautiful.

Fires are also important in limiting the growth of hardwood shrubs and trees that could eventually outcompete pines for light and space in the ab-sence of fire. Unless a fire is exceedingly hot, hardwood shrubs are usually not killed, although to all appearances they seem blackened and lifeless. Most fires burn cooler close to the ground and do not scorch the soil layer. As a result, many hardwood species resprout from still-viable roots that remain protected underground during a blaze.

Some fires in Big Cypress Swamp are caused naturally by lightning, but most are caused by humans, in the form of either arson or prescribed burns. Arson-caused fires are generally put out as soon as they are detected, but prescribed burns have become an important resource management tool for park managers. The benefits of fires were well known to Florida's early native Americans, who often initiated blazes to improve hunting, chase away bothersome insects, keep their travel corridors open, and prevent wildfires from threatening their villages. Early settlers also used fire to keep land open for pastures and agriculture. Park managers today use prescribed fires to accomplish a variety of objectives within selected areas. These objectives can include maintaining a fire-dependent community, restoring a fire-dependent community that has been changed by lack of fire, and reducing a buildup of fuel to limit the size and damage of wildfires. Dead limbs, pine needles, and brush are considered fuel that could produce an uncontrolled wildfire if too much is allowed to accumulate. Biologists may also prescribe fires to improve habitat for wildlife, help control exotic plant species, or manage for endangered species.

Prescribed fires in Big Cypress National Preserve are conducted primarily during the late spring and early summer. These fires often burn in irregular mosaic patterns, which enable wild creatures to escape from flames. The unburned patches that remain after a fire create an "edge" that provides cover, forage, and nesting habitat for birds and wildlife, in addition to serving as a seed base for revegetating burned areas.

Biologists use computer models with established parameters based on weather conditions and a set of fire objectives to determine whether to go ahead as planned with a scheduled burn. The computerized information allows them to determine what a fire will do under various conditions, which is why the phrase "burn by prescription" is used. If conditions fall outside the parameters established by the model selected for a particular burn, then the fire is canceled. Occasionally, natural features such as old pine snags used by woodpeckers, flying squirrels, or other wildlife must be protected from being damaged by prescribed burns. In such a case, the immediate area around a cavity tree is cleared to prevent fire from possibly destroying the tree or killing its inhabitants. Fire lanes and roadside vegetation are mowed to prevent fires from jumping these firebreaks. Research plots and residences are likewise protected by clearing the area of brush, dried grasses, and other fuels.

Pinelands as Wildlife Habitat

Pinelands are crucial habitat for a wide variety of wildlife in Big Cypress Swamp. Because pinelands offer fairly dry land throughout much of the year, most of the burrowing, litter-dwelling, and ground-nesting animals are found here. The openness of pinelands allows plenty of sunlight to reach the forest floor, important for such creatures as snakes and lizards which must sun in order to maintain high body temperatures. The understory of shrubs and palmettos provides patches of dense vegetation for cover-loving species, and the grasses and herbs provide consistent forage for pineland vegetarians. Pine forests are critical for birds such as the chuck-will's-widow, common nighthawk, red-cockaded woodpecker, purple martin, brown-headed nuthatch, eastern bluebird, eastern meadowlark, and Bachman's sparrow. It is also essential habitat for the six-lined racerunner, eastern coachwhip snake, scarlet kingsnake, gray fox, and endangered fox squirrel. Fox squirrels in particular prefer frequently burned pinelands with an open understory because it is easy for them to gather food and then scurry up nearby trees if danger approaches. White-tailed deer are common, and for this reason, open pinelands are a preferred hunting area for Florida panthers.

Old-growth pinelands are rare in Big Cypress Swamp for the same reasons that so few areas of old-growth cypress exist. Extensive logging in the early part of the century practically wiped them out. However, Big Cypress National Preserve has the largest area of old-growth south Florida slash pine forest remaining in southern Florida and for this reason boasts the southernmost red-cockaded woodpecker colony in the United States. Red-cockaded woodpeckers are highly social birds that live in clans, which are groups of two to nine individuals centered around one breeding pair. The nonbreeding birds in the clan are helpers that assist in incubating eggs, feeding young, making new cavities, and defending the clan's territory from other red-cockaded woodpeckers. A single clan's territory may cover as much as 100 acres of pineland or pine forest mixed with small to medium-sized hardwoods. Most of the territory is used as foraging area around the clan's colony, which is a group of cavity trees used for roosting and nesting. One to as many as twelve trees may be used for cavity trees at any one time by the woodpeckers.

Cavities are excavated in live, mature pines infected with red heart disease, which is a common heart rot fungus that causes a softening of pine heartwood. Pines are only susceptible to the fungus when they are more than sixty years old. Red-cockaded woodpeckers prefer these trees because the softened heartwood makes cavity excavation easier. Cavities within the colony may be in various stages of completion: some may be occupied, some are under construction, and still others have been abandoned. It is essential to the clan's survival that enough mature pines are available to be used for cavity trees as existing cavity trees die or are abandoned.

Unfortunately, the primary cause of the decline of red-cockaded woodpeckers is loss of habitat, namely the large stands of mature pines in which they nest and feed. This loss of old-growth pinelands is blamed for the decline of several other species in southern Florida as well, including eastern bluebirds, brown-headed nuthatches, and resident American kestrels. However, over time, as more of the pine forests within Big Cypress Swamp mature, the increased amount of suitable habitat should benefit the red-cockaded woodpeckers and other species, and populations should increase.

Another high-profile endangered species that commonly uses pinelands for hunting is the Florida panther. Florida panthers are a smaller, darker subspecies of the eastern cougar and were once common predators throughout Florida and into surrounding southern states. Now they number fewer than fifty individuals and are confined primarily to southwest Florida, where they continue to dwindle due to collisions with cars, mercury poisoning, feline diseases, and other problems.

Adult Florida panthers are solitary animals that generally only associate with each other during breeding. However, even though their home ranges are extremely large, territories may overlap considerably. Females space themselves according to how much prey is available, while males try to incorporate as many females into their home range as possible. Because male panthers play no role in raising kittens and females may come into heat at any time of year, a male panther can increase his chances of siring offspring by regularly checking the reproductive status of females whose territories are included within his own. Both male and female panthers leave "scrapes" and other scented markings as signals of their presence, sex, and reproductive status. These signs may serve to keep the panthers from crowding each other, yet still allow them to keep tabs on who their neighbors are.

Most panther conceptions occur from November through March. Generally, when a male and female form a pair, they stay together for about two weeks, during which time they mate frequently. The male ends the relationship by leaving the area. Kittens are born three months after conception and may stay with their mother for as long as two years. Panther kittens are most vulnerable during their first six months, which is when they are most likely to meet with accidents or fall prey to predators, including male panthers.

With so few panthers remaining, lack of genetic variability is a crippling factor in the panther's long-term recovery. Researchers believe that the Florida panther's genetic isolation from other panther populations may be responsible for some of the distinctive characteristics of this subspecies, including a cowlick in the middle of the back; white flecking in the fur of the head, neck, and shoulders; and a crook in the tail, which is caused by an abnormality in the last three tail vertebrae. Captive breeding programs have been implemented to help boost the number of panthers and improve their genetic diversity. Injured cats that would not survive if returned to the wild have been used in this breeding program, but so far breeding with the existing cats has been unsuccessful. Other programs have been proposed, including a controversial plan involving the removal of panther kittens from the wild to use them for new breeding stock. Regardless of what is done to increase the number of captive panthers, unanswered questions remain. What will happen when it's time to release those cats or their offspring back into the wild? More important, where will the panthers go?

As with the red-cockaded woodpecker and so many other endangered species, loss of habitat is considered the most serious threat to the long-term stability and growth of Florida panther populations. Radio telemetry studies have shown that a single panther may require a home territory ranging anywhere from 100 to 400 square miles. Although panthers do use cypress swamps and wet prairies, they seem to prefer drier upland areas of hammocks and pinelands, which offer more suitable habitat for deer and wild hogs, the panthers' primary prey. However, most of the protected land in southern Florida is comprised of wetlands, and emphasis continues to be placed on acquiring more wetlands rather than upland habitat. With the continued growth of Naples and Fort Myers to the west of Big Cypress Swamp and conversion of land from cattle ranches to citrus farms in panther habitat to the north, the amount of upland areas suitable for these animals continues to shrink. As a result, there is little room for young panthers attempting to spread out and claim new territories. Without an aggressive program designed to protect panther habitat through acquisition, conservation easements, or education of private landowners, captive breeding and other programs intended to increase panther populations will be of little benefit to the species' long-term prospects in the wild.

BIG CYPRESS SWAMP—A LIVING PATCHWORK

Cypress swamps, marshes, wet prairies, hardwood hammocks, pinelands— these are the major pieces in the patchwork of natural systems that make up Big Cypress Swamp. They are linked hydrologically by their shared need for life-giving water and biologically by the flow of plant and animal life among them. The degradation of any of these systems negatively impacts the others, and the entire swamp suffers as a result. Big Cypress Swamp's living patchwork is already somewhat frayed by the loss of such species as the ivory-billed woodpecker, Carolina parakeet, and red wolf. Have we learned enough from the extinction of these creatures to prevent the disappearance of wood storks, panthers, and other endangered animals and plants? What does the future hold for Big Cypress Swamp itself?

Unfortunately, much of Big Cypress's future is linked to human activity in the region. Encroaching development from the west and intensive agriculture from the north may threaten both the quality and the quantity of water flowing through Big Cypress and into the Ten Thousand Islands. What might be the outcome? A particularly tragic case study could be made from similar circumstances in southeast Florida, where more than seventy years of short-sighted water management projects, urban sprawl, and large-scale agriculture have nearly ruined the Kissimmee River–Lake Okeechobee–Everglades watershed. A flurry of lawsuits within the last ten years, including one by the federal government requiring the state to enforce its own water quality standards, were necessary to produce plans for a cleanup that is expected to take decades to complete and will cost taxpayers and agriculture millions of dollars. The destruction wrought on the Everglades cannot be repeated in southwest Florida. Big Cypress Swamp is simply much too precious to risk losing.

CHAPTER 2

MANGROVE SWAMPS AND
THE TEN THOUSAND ISLANDS

SPRAWLED BETWEEN THE dense mangrove swamps of Florida's south-west coast and the open waters of the Gulf of Mexico lies a tangled mass of islands, oyster bars, sandy spits, and other bits of land. Frigate birds float effortlessly in an azure sky. A school of tarpon rolls and then slips below the surface of the shallow waters. This is the Ten Thousand Islands, a region steeped both in natural history and in human lore. Although the name given to the region is somewhat misleading—there are hundreds of islands as opposed to thousands—the seemingly endless maze of channels, islands, and bays, as well as the astounding diversity and abundance of living things, have been reason enough to justify the exaggerated description. The names of many of the islands themselves reflect the area's rich ecological heritage: Panther Key, Cormorant Key, Turtle Key, Mosquito Key, Plover Key, Sandfly Island. In this fecund estuarine environment, the tides are the pulse of life, and nearly every plant and animal living in the Ten Thousand Islands is influenced by them in some way.

NATURAL FORCES THAT SHAPE THE ISLANDS

Constant change best describes the nature of the forces that shape the sandy beaches and mangrove swamps of the Ten Thousand Islands. Storms, wave action, currents, and other environmental factors constantly work to shape and reshape these communities. Sand is deposited by wave action and washed away again by storms. Channels form, silt over, and eventually disappear. The islands themselves "migrate" on their ever-shifting foundations; some move seaward toward the Gulf of Mexico, others landward toward the mangrove swamps of the coast.

Overall, the estuarine wilderness surrounding the Ten Thousand Islands covers nearly 200,000 acres from Cape Romano south to Lostman's Island. Fresh water flowing from the sloughs and rivers draining the Big Cypress Swamp mixes with salt water from the Gulf of Mexico to create the unique conditions necessary to support an astonishing array of life that thrives among oyster bars, mangrove islands, tidal mud flats, and seagrass beds—the most prominent features of the estuaries. This habitat provides vital refuge, feeding areas, and nursery grounds for southern Florida's aquatic creatures. More than 90 percent of the species considered valuable for commercial or sport purposes spend some part of their lives in these protected shallow waters.

Perhaps one of the most fascinating dimensions of this wilderness is the often-hidden intertidal realm, unveiled by low tide. At low tide, vast expanses of the shallow intertidal zone are exposed, inviting hours of exploration of mangrove roots, mud flats, tidal pools, and oyster bars. An evening walk over the flats may reveal to a careful observer nine-armed starfish, netted sea stars, spider crabs and hermit crabs, auger snails, sea hares, lettered olives, Florida cone shells, anemones, lightning whelks, heart cockles, and other living creatures on the prowl in their natural habitat. Sanderlings, willets, and plovers twitter softly in the darkness as they probe the flats for small crustaceans and other morsels.

Among the roots of red mangroves and rocky tidal pools, crown conchs, spotted mangrove crabs, sand and mud fiddler crabs, mangrove periwinkles, coon oysters, and even banded anemones and brown spiny sea stars are common. Raccoons wander through the root systems looking for horseshoe crabs stranded by the departed tide. The raccoons fare well, too, especially after a high spring tide when many of the horseshoes become trapped under roots or are left high and dry among the black mangroves. They prefer the tenderest parts of the crabs and leave the carapaces littering the sand like empty dinner plates.

What makes the abundance and variety of living things in these intertidal regions even more amazing is the environmental stress to which they are subjected. Not only must many intertidal plants and animals contend with being alternately covered and uncovered by sea water, but water temperature, salinity, dissolved oxygen, and turbidity can fluctuate wildly, creating additional hardship. Those living things that cannot withstand such extremes quickly disappear.

The small, brownish coffee-bean snail is one example of an animal caught between the two tidal worlds. Commonly found scouring red mangrove roots and leaf litter for detritus at low tide, this air-breathing snail will drown if submerged. When the tide comes in, the snail climbs the mangrove roots until it is above the tide line and waits for the tide to recede before descending once again to feed. Other animals such as tubeworms, which are incapable of moving to escape tidal influences, seal themselves in their tubes with a supply of sea water to moisten their gills until the high tide returns.

MANGROVES AND OYSTER BARS

The Ten Thousand Islands, most of them shaped like pieces of a jigsaw puzzle, are covered primarily by mangroves. Some of the islands are large and heavily forested, often rimmed by brilliant white quartz sand beaches lined with stretches of gnarled buttonwood trees. Other islands are nothing more than a few young mangroves perched as spidery growths on the backs of oyster bars and shoals. Channels snake between the islands, occasionally branching into smaller, narrower channels to form confusing labyrinths. Many of the channels lead to wide bays, where bottle-nosed dolphins suddenly spout, linger near the surface, and then disappear. Ospreys scream from their massive nests wedged in the crowns of large black or red mangroves.

Other smaller, canopied channels, bathed in a green glow from light filtered through the interlacing tangle of mangrove branches overhead, lead to quiet backwater lakes. On calm days, the silence in these backwater lakes is almost absolute, broken only by an occasional croak from a night heron roosting in the mangroves or the crashing of a snook chasing finger mullet through shallows among the mangrove roots. On the outer fringes of the islands, mullet, redfish, sea trout, and other fish cruise the channels between oyster bars, waiting for food caught up in the current.

Mangroves and oysters have been instrumental in the creation and continued development of the sinuous network of islands and channels so characteristic of the region. Longshore currents from the north carry quartz sand, depositing it in deeper water parallel to the shore of the mainland. As the sand accumulates, it rises nearer the surface. If water conditions and the flow of currents are favorable, oysters begin to colonize the sand deposits, adding their limestone shells to the upward growth of the sediments. Eventually, the accumulation of sand and oysters reaches the intertidal zone near the surface, where the oysters are exposed at low tide, creating an oyster bar.

Oyster bars frequently become quite extensive and develop at right angles to tidal currents in order to take advantage of the steady supply of nutrients. Smaller, winding branches extend at intervals from the oyster bed's main line of growth, often meeting and forming small lakes and bays. Red mangrove seedlings borne on the tide take root in sediments that have become trapped on the oyster bar. Over time, the mangroves engulf the oyster bar and form an island of roots and leaves. The red mangroves' distinctive arching prop roots trap and stabilize waterborne sediments and other materials, adding the material needed to continue the development and growth of the island. It is these spidery prop roots and the manner in which the trees seem to march out across the shallow intertidal zone beyond the oyster bar that inspired the Seminoles to describe red mangroves as "Walking Trees." As the mangroves continue to spread, the islands grow and the channels become smaller, restricting the tidal currents upon which the oysters depend to bring them nutrients. As a result, the oysters gradually die out, leaving their limestone shell base as mute testimony of their role in the islands' development.

Three types of mangroves can be found in the Ten Thousand Islands. Red mangroves, the most abundant species, are found within dense mangrove swamps, often on the outer exposed edges, as well as in isolated clumps on small sand spits. They are the pioneer trees, the primary builders of the mangrove swamps. To survive the salty conditions of their estuarine environment, red mangroves prevent too much salt from entering their arching root systems by separating fresh water from salt at the root surface. Through a reverse osmosis process powered by high negative pressure in the xylem resulting from transpiration at the leaf surface, they literally exclude salt from their roots. What little salt a tree assimilates is stored in the leaves and is removed when the leaves die and fall off. Black mangroves, noted for their radial root systems and pencil-like, woody pneumatophores that stick straight up from the mud, prefer areas within the swamps that are more sheltered from wind and wave action. As with the arching roots of the red mangroves, the pneumatophores of the black mangrove allow the tree to aerate during low tide. White mangroves prefer slightly higher, drier ground than the red and black mangroves and are often found mixed in with buttonwoods. Buttonwoods, although not true mangroves, are salt-tolerant trees common to most mangrove swamps. Their gnarled, textured bark makes them ideal platforms for orchids, bromeliads, and other epiphytic plants. Black mangroves, white mangroves, and buttonwoods take up salt water through their roots, but exude excess salt through glands in the petiole at the base of each fleshy leaf.

The energy base of the incredible mangrove ecosystem and surrounding coastal systems is the mangrove leaf itself. Although a mangrove leaf obviously benefits the mangrove while it is alive on the tree, it is not until the leaf dies that its energy is unlocked and used by the rest of the food chain. Mangrove leaves die and sprout a few at a time, unlike the needles of cypress that sprinkle down in autumn and burst forth again in spring. Three-and-a-half tons of mangrove leaves per acre per year are dropped, which means that a steady supply of nutrients is available to the mangrove swamp throughout the year.

When a mangrove leaf falls into the water, it begins a long process of decomposition. First, the tannic acid must leach out of the leaf, which may take up to five weeks. The release of tannic acid is what stains the water in the Ten Thousand Islands its typical greenish to reddish-brown color. Once the tannic acid is gone, the leaf is attacked by microscopic fungi, protozoa, and bacteria, which coat it and begin to break it down into organic compounds, minerals, carbon dioxide, and nitrogenous waste. Amphipods and small herbivorous animals such as crabs help the decomposition process along by shredding the leaves into tiny, partially decomposed bits called detritus. The detritus drifts with the tide, providing food for sea worms, marine snails, shrimp, and crabs—creatures at the bottom of the food chain. Minnows and small fish feed on these invertebrates and in turn become food for larger fish. Mullet are among the few large adult fish that feed directly on detritus. Schools of these silvery fish provide a fundamental source of food for the ecosystem's major predators, such as snook and tarpon, as well as bottle-nosed dolphins, brown pelicans, ospreys, and bald eagles.

How red mangroves produce seedlings is as fascinating as their other unique characteristics. Rather than dropping dormant seeds into the water or mud, red mangroves retain their fleshy propagules (the mangrove equivalent to a seed) until they have germinated and developed into eight-to-ten-inch-long, cigar-shaped seedlings. Only then do the seedlings drop into the mud beneath the parent tree or fall into the water to be carried away by the tide. Red mangrove seedlings can survive for up to a year bobbing on ocean currents; in fact, this ability to travel is one reason for their wide distribution along tropical shorelines in Africa, Central and South America, and the Pacific Ocean. Black and white mangroves produce propagules as well, although the propagules of these trees are smaller and will not remain viable for as long as those of red mangroves when immersed in salt water.

During their first few days in the water, red mangrove seedlings float horizontally. Eventually, one end swells with sea water and sinks, so that the seedling bobs in an upright position. When a seedling is finally washed up on a shoal or oyster bar, the submerged end lodges in sediment, takes root, and soon sprouts green leaves from its top. Prop roots develop within a few months. As other seedlings become stranded in the same manner, the shoal or oyster bar is well on its way to becoming another mangrove island.

On many of the larger mangrove islands, enough sediment has accumulated behind the mangroves to form higher, dry sandy ground that is colonized by a variety of salt-tolerant trees, succulent plants, and grasses. Sea

Moon Rise #2

Custard Apple Swamp

Loop Road #2

Rock Island Prairie #1

Deep Lake Strand

Splendid Isolation

Tamiami Trail

Loop Road

Big Cypress Swamp #7

Thompson Pine Island Road #10

Rock Island Prairie #2

Little Pavilion Key

Thompson Pine Island Road #4

Buttonwood

Indian Key Pass

Big Cypress
Moon Rise

Tamiami Trail #3

Gaskin Bay

Loose Screw Sanctuary #2

Ochopee #3

Rock Island Prairie #4

Dog House Key

Roberts Lake Strand Buggy Trail

grape and gumbo limbo are among the largest trees growing within a tropical hammock, often reaching heights of fifty or sixty feet. Strangler fig, mastic, stoppers, cabbage palm, wax myrtle, red bay, and gray nickerbean form dense thickets on some islands.

SAND DUNES

Closer to the beach along stretches of shoreline where the mangroves have not grown to the water's edge, wave action and wind often pile up enough sand to form low dunes. The plants that colonize the dunes are essential in capturing sand grains and holding the dunes together. Many dune plants have special sand-holding capabilities and are found in distinct zones along the dune. For example, seaside purslane and inkberry are among the beach pioneers found closest to the high tide mark. Farther up along the front edge of the dune are grasses such as sea oats, salt-marsh cordgrass, and panic grass. On the top of the dune and stretching down the dune's back edge are prickly pear cactus and Spanish bayonet, as well as shrubs like wax myrtle and the groundsel tree. These plants may then grade into a coastal thicket or tropical hammock.

Peculiar holes dimple the sand among dune grasses and black mangrove pneumatophores down to the low tide mark. These are the burrows of sand fiddlers—the ubiquitous little crab of sandy beaches throughout the Ten Thousand Islands and southwestern Florida. The entrance around each burrow is surrounded by small balls of sand, which represent the remains of past meals. Sand fiddlers feed by straining sand to remove detritus, leaving balls of cleaned sand as a result. These are then rolled out of the burrow at low tide when the entrance to the burrow is exposed. As the tide begins to come in, the fiddlers retreat to their burrows, plug the entrances, and wait until the next low tide before venturing out once again.

Male sand fiddlers sport one very large claw and a smaller claw used for feeding. The large claw is primarily a mating tool. When advertising for a mate, a male sand fiddler crouches outside his burrow and waves his large claw high overhead. This claw waving attracts not only females from neighboring burrows, but also an occasional rival male. Clashes between males result in lots of claw waving and sporadic jousting, but no damage to either contestant.

Mud fiddler crabs, which live on the tidal mud flats and among the roots of red mangroves, are about the same size as sand fiddlers, but darker. They too live in burrows and exhibit the same behavior as their sand-dwelling cousins. At low tide, vast rafts of mud fiddlers swarm across the flats in search of food, their claws and legs clicking against shells and rocks as they move. With the exception of crabs, most of the creatures that live on the mud flats and sand bars in the Ten Thousand Islands spend their lives beneath the surface. These include clams, mud snails, worms, and brittle stars. Immature pink shrimp, white shrimp, and nearly transparent grass shrimp are tiny creatures that are well camouflaged and—although they do not bury themselves in sediment—only rarely seen.

SEAGRASS BEDS

Out past the intertidal zone in slightly deeper water are beds of seagrasses, dominated by turtle grass. Turtle grass—a true flowering grass—is a favorite food of green sea turtles, hence its common name. This species does best in areas protected from surf action and wind-driven currents, which explains why there are so many large, healthy beds throughout the sheltered waters of the Ten Thousand Islands. The half-inch-wide blades of turtle grass provide the perfect anchoring surface for no fewer than 113 species of algae and several species of sponges, hydrozoan polyps, flatworms, and tunicates. Shrimp, spider and hermit crabs, Jamaican lucine clams, lightning and fig whelks, sea cucumbers, and starfish are common invertebrate residents in the turtle grass beds.

The abundance of tiny creatures and the sheltering blades of grass attract a wide variety of fish to the seagrass beds. Bait fish such as ballyhoo and needlefish are common; however, the speckled sea trout, pompano, permit, flounder, and other game fish are what draw fishermen to the seagrass beds on a regular basis. Birds, including ospreys, bald eagles, magnificent frigate birds, and brown pelicans, appreciate the bounty in the turtle grass as well.

Among the most noticeable residents of the Ten Thousand Islands system are members of its insect population—the black salt-marsh mosquito and biting midges. Black salt-marsh mosquitoes, distinguished by dark bands on their legs, are only one out of approximately forty species of mosquitoes found in the Ten Thousand Islands and Big Cypress Swamp. Only the female mosquitoes seek out meals of blood to provide protein for developing eggs. Males feed on plant juices and flower nectar.

Black salt-marsh mosquitoes gather in swarms at dawn and dusk to find mates, retreating to the shady interiors of hammocks and mangrove swamps during the day. Females lay their eggs in the mud among mangrove roots or near shallow, still pools flushed by the tide. After the eggs hatch, the larvae, or wigglers, feed on bacteria and microbes, and many in turn fall prey to killifish and other small aquatic predators. Depending on the season, two or more weeks may pass before the thousands of surviving larvae emerge as adults, ready to breed and repeat the cycle. In typical summer weather, adult mosquitoes have about a month in which to breed before they die.

Biting midges, also known as sandflies, punkies, and "no-see-ums," look like mere specks when they land on your skin, although they make up in biting power what they may lack in size. Three species of voracious midges plague residents and visitors to the southwest coast throughout the year; however, January and February are generally the months in which these "jaws with wings" are least troublesome. As with black salt-marsh mosquitoes, dawn and dusk are periods of peak activity for biting midges, and it is only the females that bite and take blood to nourish their eggs. Anywhere from 25 to 110 eggs may be produced from a two-to-five-minute blood meal, depending on the species, the size of the female, and how much blood she has taken. Eggs are laid in wet mud in saltwater marshes and among mangroves, where they hatch into predacious larvae that live in the mud and feed on other small organisms. Depending on the species, a biting midge's total life span can range from a few weeks to as long as several months, with the majority of that time spent in the larval stage.

Abundant food and the unspoiled habitat found within the Ten Thousand Islands are primary reasons why more than 300 species of birds are either permanent residents or pass through during seasonal migrations. Within the recesses of the mangrove swamps, migratory warblers, cardinals, great crested flycatchers, pileated woodpeckers, and red-bellied woodpeckers are common. Thousands of shorebirds congregate on sandbars and exposed mud flats throughout the year to feed, roost, and nest. During the winter months, the number of shorebirds swells with an influx of seasonal residents, such as semipalmated plovers, piping plovers, sanderlings, dunlins, and dowitchers.

Swallow-tailed kites, summer residents in the Ten Thousand Islands, are more likely to terrorize small creatures in the tops of the mangroves than shorebirds on the flats. These graceful, fork-tailed white and black raptors pluck lizards and snakes from the treetops and eat them on the wing. The kites winter in South America and return to southern Florida in late February to nest. The sight of the spiraling ascents and sudden dips of their aerial courtship ritual, sometimes with one bird carrying a branch in its talons, is an experience to remember for a lifetime.

Perhaps the bird most symbolic of the Ten Thousand Islands is the osprey. Year-round residents, ospreys can nearly always be seen wheeling over a promising stretch of water, pulling up to hover in midair as if gauging the distance to their quarry, and then suddenly dropping into the water feet first, like a feathered stone. Before the spray even clears, the osprey is airborne, quivering to shake the water from its feathers as it clutches a sea trout or mullet tightly in its talons. As early as December, ospreys begin gathering branches to reinforce the immense nests they have constructed in the tops of tall mangroves and on channel markers. The birds frequently use the same nests year after year, adding more sticks to the bulky mass in each new nesting season.

After mating, the female lays two to three eggs, which she incubates for thirty days. The eggs hatch three days apart, meaning that the first chick will have a head start on its siblings. In tough years when fishing is not good, there is intense rivalry among chicks for food, and the youngest, smallest chick does not always survive. Young ospreys spend seven to eight weeks in their nestling stage and then another two months as fledglings. Within two months after fledging, they are able to catch their own fish, apparently without any training from the adults.

Isolated mangrove islands found in shallow bays in dense mainland swamps, in addition to the mangrove keys in the Ten Thousand Islands, provide important nesting habitat for herons, egrets, white ibis, pelicans, and cormorants. Rogers River Bay Rookery is among the most productive rookeries in southwest Florida. Indian Key and Cormorant Key contain small but consistent rookeries. Egrets, herons, and ibis nesting in the mangroves generally begin to breed in late spring and early summer, almost three months later than their counterparts nesting in freshwater areas of Big Cypress Swamp and the Everglades. These mangrove-nesting wading birds utilize freshwater and saltwater marshes, as well as the intertidal zone among the mangrove roots, for feeding themselves and their hungry chicks. However, as with freshwater rookeries, too much water or too little water in the marshes can spell ruin for the success of wading bird rookeries in the mangroves.

Cormorants and brown pelicans nesting in the Ten Thousand Islands generally fish the estuaries and open waters of the Gulf of Mexico, insulating them to some degree from vagaries in water levels of interior wetlands. However, they have their own unique problems. Because mullet and other fish low in the food chain are a mainstay of their diet, any declines in the populations of these fish directly affect them. This means that if mullet are commercially overharvested or an oil spill in the Gulf of Mexico kills off large numbers of fish, the pelicans and cormorants will be among the first victims of the crisis. Strong storms can devastate rookeries on exposed islands, and discarded monofilament fishing line, which so often ends up in mangrove branches, entangles and kills many nestlings and adult birds.

MAMMALS

The Ten Thousand Islands are home to several mammal species, but with the exception of raccoons, people are most likely to see only West Indian manatees and bottle-nosed dolphins. Manatees are immense, slow-moving, more or less seal-shaped, water-dwelling mammals with broad, flat, rounded tails. They range in color from light gray to brown, and large adult females may reach lengths of nearly thirteen feet and weigh well over a ton. Their small, wide-set eyes and stiff whiskers sprouting from their bulbous faces give them a lovable, placid look. The West Indian manatee, which generally ranges from Florida to northern South America, belongs to the order Sirenia, of which there are two other species worldwide. Manatees in the Ten Thousand Islands graze on the fringes of seagrass beds where there is quick access to deeper water. They are extremely susceptible to cold and may be killed by a sharp drop in water temperature.

Manatees have virtually no natural enemies other than humans. For thousands of years, they were hunted for meat, bone, hides, and fat by Indians and later for meat and hides by nineteenth-century pioneers. Today, manatees are protected by law, yet more than 30 percent of the more than 100 manatee deaths reported each year are related to human activities. Power boats are the single most common cause of manatee deaths, which is why boaters need to exercise extreme caution when running the protected bays and channels among the islands. Most adult manatees bear scars from encounters with boat propellers. Considering that manatees reproduce very slowly (females typically give birth to a single calf every four or five years) and that the current manatee population is estimated at only 1,200 to 1,500 animals, it seems the only feasible manatee recovery plan is to sharply reduce the number of manatee deaths that occur each year. By setting aside manatee refuges and sanctuaries, enforcing boat speed limits, educating the public, and protecting aquatic habitat, we can help manatees to prosper and remain an enduring part of the Ten Thousand Islands.

Bottle-nosed dolphins are most often seen when they venture into bays and shallow water along the coast or swim beside boats in the channels. Dolphins also occasionally cruise up the rivers and into the inland bays, where they delight canoeists paddling through the backcountry. These intelligent relatives of whales love mullet and will charge into the middle of a big school, creating an unbelievable fracas as water froths white and frantic mullet leap in all directions. Mullet are tossed into the air and then caught and swallowed before they hit the water. The effortless grace the dolphins exhibit when a small group of them arch their dorsal fins against the sparkling, backlit waters of Gaskin Bay is among the most exhilarating scenes you can witness in the Ten Thousand Islands.

HURRICANES

Mangroves and the many other life forms in the Ten Thousand Islands are well adapted to the stressful conditions of their estuarine home. However, sudden environmental changes, such as those brought about by hurricanes, can cause serious damage. Since their first tenuous beginnings, these mangrove swamps have weathered hurricanes. Hurricane-force winds can uproot even large mangroves and cause high, powerful waves that severely erode shorelines accustomed to typically gentle (what marine researchers call "low-energy") wave action from the Gulf. The storm surges often associated with hurricanes produce a mixed bag of benefits and damage, including severe bottom and coastal erosion, recycling of bay sediments and nutrients, an influx of new nutrients and sediments from adjacent waters, and a redistribution of bottom sediments. Seagrass communities are altered or destroyed in the process. Torrential rains from hurricanes can reduce the salinity of isolated bays and introduce sediments and nutrients through runoff from the mainland.

Hurricane Donna in 1960 and Hurricane Andrew in 1992 destroyed large areas of the mature southern mangrove swamp in Everglades National Park. With Donna, winds reached a sustained velocity of 140 miles per hour, with frequent gusts up to 180 miles per hour. Storm tides rose twelve feet above normal and a drift line of debris eight feet high formed along the coast. Within the Ten Thousand Islands region, 10 to 25 percent of the mature mangroves were killed. South of the Ten Thousand Islands, the percentage of trees killed reached 75 percent. Donna also wiped out most of the vegetation on Duck Rock, which before the storm had been a roosting spot for as many as 100,000 white ibis, as well as great egrets, several species of herons, brown pelicans, cormorants, and more than 300 roseate spoonbills. Half of the white ibis population was believed to have been lost in the storm, and the remaining birds attempted to roost on Duck Rock for two years before abandoning it for more suitable sites on other islands.

HUMAN IMPACT

Hurricanes may cause serious initial damage to mangrove and estuarine ecosystems, but they rebound with increased vigor, much like freshwater marshes and pinelands after a fire. The real danger to the continued survival of the Ten Thousand Islands comes not from natural events but from human activities.

Human beings have had a long history in the Ten Thousand Islands. Supported by the abundance of fish and wildlife, the first Indian settlements developed on the islands almost 2,000 years ago. Shell mounds, created by the Calusa Indians in part to produce high, dry land that would not flood during high storm tides and hurricanes, have survived for centuries and are still visible today on some of the larger islands. Tropical hardwoods colonized these mounds and on many islands created hammocks. The soil beneath the hammocks, although thin, is the richest to be found on the islands. Unfortunately, that very richness doomed many hammocks by attracting homesteaders who cleared them for farming in the late 1800s and early 1900s. Crops usually did well until storm tides swept over a homesteader's island, leaving the soil too salty for farming. The homesteader and his family would then move to another island, clear trees to plant crops, and start over.

By the early 1900s, there was little evidence of the incredible numbers and variety of wildlife that had attracted settlers in the first place. The tremendous rookeries of herons, egrets, and roseate spoonbills were plundered and almost completely wiped out by 1915 to supply the plume trade. Alligators were butchered for their hides by the tens of thousands. Otters, panthers, red wolves, and black bears suffered a similar fate. Red wolves are now extinct in Florida and panthers nearly so. As wildlife dwindled, hunters turned to fishing and clamming. The clamming industry has died out, and within the last ten years stocks of redfish and mullet have crashed due to commercial overfishing. Redfish can now only be taken recreationally, and commercial mullet fishing within Everglades National Park is prohibited.

Over and above the stresses on fish stocks, there is the constant threat of an oil spill along the southwest Florida coast. Fear of a spill has been so great that legislation was passed in 1990 imposing a twelve-year moratorium on offshore oil drilling along the southwest coast of Florida. There still remains the risk of a tanker spill, but new standards for tanker safety—if they are enforced—should reduce the chances of oil ever touching the Florida coastline.

Despite these challenges and the past assaults on its resources, the Ten Thousand Islands region remains a place of subtle beauty and remarkable vitality. Two-thirds of the islands lie within the boundaries of Everglades National Park. The state of Florida maintains the Cape Romano–Ten Thousand Islands Aquatic Preserve to protect those islands and surrounding waters that lie outside national park boundaries. Perhaps, with continued preservation, this estuarine wilderness will stay as it is—wild and unspoiled, an extraordinary place to experience the ebb and flow of life on nature's terms.

CHAPTER 3

THE CHALLENGE
OF PRESERVATION

𝒯HE BIG CYPRESS SWAMP WATERSHED is one of the most pristine wild systems in Florida, in spite of a history of past human abuses. Widespread logging, commercial hunting and fishing, and drainage for development and agriculture made their impact, but the system is making a remarkable recovery under the combined protection of federal agencies, state agencies, and private conservation groups. More than one million acres of the watershed are currently preserved in Everglades National Park, Big Cypress National Preserve, Florida Panther National Wildlife Refuge, Collier-Seminole State Park, Fakahatchee Strand State Preserve, Cape Romano–Ten Thousand Islands Aquatic Preserve, and the National Audubon Society's Corkscrew Swamp Sanctuary. Its surface waters have been designated as an "Outstanding Florida Water" by state law and are protected against degradation of water quality. Federal and state laws designed to protect wetland habitat also help to limit the destruction of areas currently not under public or private conservation ownership.

In spite of these safeguards, pressing concerns still remain. Southwest Florida is one of the fastest-growing areas in the United States, and the escalating human population places increasing pressure on the Big Cypress watershed. Development is spreading east from Naples and Fort Myers, and the citrus industry is advancing south from central Florida to the northern edges of Big Cypress National Preserve. As a result, undeveloped land becomes more scarce and extremely expensive to purchase for conservation purposes.

More people in the region also means that there is increased pressure on the watershed to supply fresh water for human needs, leaving less water for wildlife and disrupting water-dependent natural systems. Park boundaries in themselves can do nothing to prevent the degradation of protected resources by contaminants originating from surrounding developed areas. They can do nothing to ensure that historic flow conditions will be maintained in the watershed. Although wetlands are protected by law, loopholes exist and, as a result, wetlands disappear. Upland habitat, such as pinelands and hammocks, does not even enjoy the scant regulatory protection afforded to wetlands and is typically the most desirable for development. Only public awareness of the problems and public support for measures designed to safeguard the natural environment will guarantee long-term protection of this precious wilderness.

Big Cypress Swamp and the Ten Thousand Islands are becoming increasingly popular for outdoor enthusiasts, as well as casual tourists, who want to experience one of the best remaining examples of the "real Florida." To retain the land's wild character, parks and preserves are managed so that natural processes contributing to the region's unique characteristics remain intact. This often involves prescribed burning and the removal of non-native (exotic) species, such as melaleuca, Brazilian pepper, and Australian pine. Wild hogs are an exotic species in Big Cypress Swamp, but because they have become an important prey animal for Florida panthers, no eradication programs (with the exception of seasonal hunting in game areas) have been mounted against them.

Interpretive and recreational opportunities for the public are also high management priorities, although the types of activities available vary from park to park. For example, hunting and the recreational use of off-road vehicles (ORVs) and airboats are restricted to specific areas within Big Cypress National Preserve because of their impact on wildlife and other natural resources. The size of interpretive facilities, number of developed hiking or canoe trails, and type of concessioner services will also vary among parks. Some parks provide developed camping facilities; some don't. To help you better understand the similarities and differences among the major parks in

Big Cypress Swamp and the Ten Thousand Islands, the natural features, history, management priorities, and recreational/interpretive activities have been highlighted for each one. If you are planning a visit, use this information as a guide to make your experience more rewarding.

EVERGLADES NATIONAL PARK

Over the last century, many people have recognized the importance of southern Florida's wildlands and the need to protect them, even as significant portions were being torn asunder by flood control projects, agriculture, development, and logging operations. Among the earliest and most influential visionaries was landscape architect Ernest F. Coe, who in 1928 began working toward his dream of seeing the Everglades become a national park. Although not officially established as a national park until 1947, a bill authorizing lands to be acquired for the park was passed by Congress in 1934. More than a decade passed before the nearly 1,400,000 acres that originally comprised the park (Everglades now covers 1,506,539 acres) were finally allocated and private land within its boundaries could be purchased. On December 6, 1947, Everglades National Park was officially dedicated by President Harry Truman in a ceremony held at Everglades City. The park's management principles have retained much of the intent of the original congressional act of May 10, 1934, that no development in the park or services for visitors be allowed to interfere with the preservation of "unique flora and fauna and the essential primitive natural conditions now prevailing in this area." National park policy also maintains that the park must be managed for the benefit of entire ecosystems rather than individual species. In 1978, much of the park, including a significant portion of the Ten Thousand Islands, was declared legislative wilderness under the Wilderness Act. Everglades National Park has also been designated as an International Biosphere Reserve, a classification attesting to international recognition of its value as a biome of global significance.

Two-thirds of Everglades National Park encompasses vital coastal estuarine areas, while the remaining one-third protects freshwater systems such as sawgrass marshes and cypress heads. The Gulf Coast district of the park, which includes the Ten Thousand Islands and much of southern Florida's mangrove forest, features three primary coastal systems—mangrove forest, estuary, and coastal prairie. Indian mounds are found on some of the islands and are protected as part of the park's cultural history. Resource management responsibilities in the Gulf Coast district primarily include endangered species protection, exotic species removal (especially Australian pines and seaside mahoe), cultural resource protection, and monitoring programs for backcountry campsite use.

The Gulf Coast Ranger Station and Visitor Center on State Road 29 at Everglades City is the park's primary departure point for exploring the Ten Thousand Islands and the western portion of the mangrove forest. Fishing, boating, canoeing, and concession-operated sightseeing boat tours of the outer islands and mangrove backcountry are the main activities for visitors here. Concessioners in Everglades City rent canoes for people interested in exploring the Ten Thousand Islands or canoeing the Wilderness Waterway, which is an inland route through the bays and creeks of the mangrove swamp between Flamingo and Everglades City. Overnight canoe trips to the outer islands are popular as well; check in with the ranger station to obtain a free backcountry camping permit and site location for each night you will be out. The number of island sites is limited, and the number of people allowed at each site is also regulated to reduce human impact on the islands.

Interpretive activities for park visitors presently include displays in the visitor center, audio/visual programs, and ranger-led canoe trips and short interpretive programs during the winter. Special environmental education programs for schoolchildren in Dade and Collier counties are an important interpretive function conducted by park naturalists at the Gulf Coast Station and the Loop Road Interpretive Center in Big Cypress National Preserve. The main purpose of the environmental education camps and day trips is to instill in children a sense of responsibility for the environment in the hope that, when these children become adults and decision makers, they will have a greater appreciation for the delicate balance that must be struck between human progress and the preservation of natural features and resources. This public support will benefit park programs and ultimately the wildlands protected within the parks.

For more information about the Gulf Coast district of Everglades National Park, contact Everglades National Park, P.O. Box 120, Everglades City, FL 33929, or call (941) 695-3311. General information can be obtained by writing the park headquarters at Everglades National Park, 40001 S.R. 9336, Homestead, FL 33034-6733, or by calling (305) 242-7700.

BIG CYPRESS NATIONAL PRESERVE

Big Cypress National Preserve encompasses the heart of Big Cypress Swamp, more than 700,000 acres of it. Cypress swamps, wet prairies, freshwater marshes, pinelands, and hardwood hammocks dominate much of the landscape, although the extreme southern edge of the preserve does include a fringe of salt marshes and mangrove forest. One of its most fascinating aspects is its primitive nature and relative inaccessibility. It is also one of the few places in southern Florida where you can stand in the middle of a marsh or cypress swamp for more than fifteen minutes and hear nothing except the sounds of nature at work. No traffic, no planes, no machinery. That in itself makes the preserve a paradise.

Concern for the protection of water resources flowing into Everglades National Park and the public outcry over a proposed jetport at the northeastern edge of Big Cypress Swamp prompted the establishment of Big Cypress National Preserve by Congress in 1974. The purpose for the preserve as dictated by Public Law 93-440 is to "assure the preservation, conservation, and protection of the natural, scenic, hydrologic, floral and faunal, and recreational values of the Big Cypress Watershed in the State of Florida and to provide for the enhancement and public enjoyment thereof. . . ." The language in this act emphasizes the need to protect not only the natural system but "recreational values" as well, values which include hunting and Off-Road Vehicle (ORV) use. Although Big Cypress National Preserve is managed by the National Park Service, the preserve differs from national parks in that hunting and ORV use are permitted, in addition to limited mineral (oil and natural gas) exploration and grazing. Members of the Miccosukee and Seminole Indian tribes are also allowed to continue living and conducting traditional activities within the boundaries of the preserve.

With so many diverse and often contradictory responsibilities, preserve personnel spend most of their time carrying out the many management roles for which they are responsible. Research and management of endangered species such as the red-cockaded woodpecker and the Florida panther are a priority, especially since thirty-five native species at Big Cypress are listed as endangered, threatened, or are candidates for consideration for listing under the Endangered Species Act. Natural resource management, which includes prescribed burning and fire suppression (Big Cypress experiences the greatest fire load of any unit in the national park system), hydrological studies, monitoring of the effects of oil and gas exploration, monitoring of the effects of ORV use, and exotic plant control, is probably the most time-consuming management responsibility. The Florida Game and Fresh Water Fish Commission jointly manages game species and hunting in Big Cypress National Preserve with the National Park Service.

At the present time, few interpretive activities are available to the general public, in part because most visitors are sportsmen, ORV users, and owners of property within the preserve. However, an expanded interpretive program and additional recreational opportunities for hiking, canoeing, camping, and picnicking have been proposed and are likely to be implemented in the near future. Hiking and backcountry camping are currently allowed throughout the preserve. Several primitive camping sites are also available and can be easily accessed from U.S. 41. The South Terminus of the Florida Trail is located at the Sawmill Road intersection with Loop Road and continues north through the preserve for nearly fifty miles. Most hikers use the trail during the winter because it is cooler and drier, but contact the Oasis ranger station before your trip to check on trail conditions. Be especially careful if you plan to hike in the preserve during the gun season (which extends from October through December) because of the number of hunters pursuing deer and wild hogs.

For more information about Big Cypress National Preserve, contact Big Cypress National Preserve, HCR 61, Box 11, Ochopee, FL 33943, or call (941) 695-4111.

FLORIDA PANTHER NATIONAL WILDLIFE REFUGE

The Florida Panther National Wildlife Refuge is one of the newest units in the National Wildlife Refuge system. Unlike the national and state parks/preserves in Big Cypress Swamp, this national wildlife refuge was established in 1989 primarily to aid the recovery of a single species, the Florida panther, by protecting 24,300 acres of productive panther habitat in the northern Fakahatchee Strand. An additional 5,110 acres are scheduled to be acquired within the next several years. Although the Florida panther is the targeted benefactor of the refuge, all wildlife and plants found on the refuge are protected, including several rare and endangered species native to the Fakahatchee Strand.

The goal of the refuge's management programs is to provide ideal habitat for Florida panthers. Prescribed burning will be carried out to maintain native plant communities and ensure an abundance of white-tailed deer, their primary prey. Other programs, such as establishing food plots and wildlife clearings, will also be tested. Currently, the refuge is not open to the public in order to keep human disturbance to a minimum.

For information about scientific or educational work on the refuge, contact the refuge manager at Florida Panther National Wildlife Refuge, U.S. Fish and Wildlife Service, 2629 S. Horseshoe Drive, Naples, FL 33942, or call (941) 643-2636.

COLLIER-SEMINOLE STATE PARK

Named for the Seminole Indians, who have long made southwest Florida their home, and Barron Collier, a wealthy advertising entrepreneur and pioneer developer, Collier-Seminole State Park boasts 6,423 acres of pristine mangrove swamp, hardwood hammocks, cypress swamp, salt marshes, and pine flatwoods. The Blackwater River originates within park boundaries and flows into the Ten Thousand Islands and the Gulf of Mexico.

Collier-Seminole State Park is run by the Florida Department of Environmental Protection, Division of Recreation and Parks, which utilizes "natural systems management" in an attempt to maintain the natural communities within the park as an interrelated system rather than for the benefit of particular species. In other words, rather than focusing exclusively on the habitat needs of a few species, park managers attempt to re-create or maintain the ecosystems required by all plants and animals found within the park. Restoration and maintenance activities include exotic plant removal, prescribed burning, and hydrological restoration (which may involve filling drainage ditches and canals and removing artificial dams, dikes, and spoil mounds). Priorities within Collier-Seminole include eliminating exotic plants such as melaleuca and Brazilian pepper, restoring disturbed areas of Royal Palm Hammock, and using prescribed fires to retain the true ecological nature of the park's pineland, wet prairies, salt marshes, and other fire-dependent communities.

Collier-Seminole offers a number of recreational activities for visitors, including hiking, camping, boating, fishing, canoeing, and interpretive services. A concessioner operates a narrated boat tour along the Blackwater River and adjacent mangrove swamp. Most of the park (4,760 acres) is a mangrove swamp wilderness preserve. The preserve is accessible only by canoe, along a 13.6-mile loop trail. A primitive campsite is available for visitors who wish to stay overnight (insects permitting). For hikers in search of a wilderness experience away from the campgrounds, a 6.5-mile loop trail winds through pine flatwoods and cypress swamp; a primitive campsite is also available on this trail for overnight hikers.

One of Collier-Seminole's primary natural features is Royal Palm Hammock, a tropical hardwood hammock containing several large Florida royal palms, gumbo limbos, Jamaican dogwoods, white stoppers, and other species of tropical trees and understory growth. A self-guided nature trail winds through the hammock and connects with a boardwalk system that takes you through salt marshes, extensive stands of leather ferns, and a white mangrove swamp. A raised platform at the end of the boardwalk overlooks a large salt marsh where you may see a northern harrier searching for cotton rats and marsh rabbits, a bobcat on the prowl, or even a black bear on its way to its sleeping quarters for the day.

Local history is preserved within the park as well. The Blockhouse is a replica of an army frontier blockhouse that commemorates the efforts of U.S. soldiers in the Seminole Wars. Built during the development of the park in the late 1930s by Collier County, it served as Collier County's first museum. The park also exhibits the Bay City Walking Dredge, which was responsible for constructing the eight-mile section of the Tamiami Trail between what is now State Road 92 and State Road 951. Grocery Place, accessed by using the canoe trail, is a small area along Royal Palm Hammock Creek that has historic interest as a settlement occupied around the turn of the century.

Collier-Seminole State Park is located on U.S. 41 (Tamiami Trail), thirteen miles east of Naples. While there are plenty of plants and wildlife to see during any season of the year, you may want to call ahead, especially in the summer, to get a mosquito report. Collier-Seminole is famous for its mosquitoes, and if you arrive unprepared for them, your visit is bound to be "invigorating" at best. For more information about the park, contact Collier-Seminole State Park, Route 4, Box 848, Naples, FL 33961, or call (941) 394-3397.

FAKAHATCHEE STRAND STATE PRESERVE

Fakahatchee Strand State Preserve is a 74,000-acre preserve managed by the Florida Department of Environmental Protection, Division of Recreation and Parks. Its primary purpose is to protect the amazingly diverse variety of plant and animal life found in the Fakahatchee Strand and surrounding ecosystems and provide opportunities for recreational activities, such as nature study, hiking, and photography. Management principles are similar to those of Collier-Seminole State Park in that the preserve is maintained for the benefit of entire ecosystems rather than for individual species. Exotic plant removal and prescribed burning are among the management activities intended to allow natural communities within the preserve to retain their true ecological nature.

The Fakahatchee Strand is the largest wetland extension of Okaloacoochee Slough, which is the major natural freshwater drainage from southwestern Big Cypress Swamp into the estuarine regions of the Ten Thousand Islands. The Fakahatchee Strand is also the largest and perhaps the most unusual cypress/mixed hardwood strand in the United States. Its stand of Florida royal palms is the most extensive in the world, and it features the world's only royal palm/bald cypress forest. More varieties of orchids and bromeliads can be found here than anywhere else in the United States. At least twelve species of plants in the Fakahatchee Strand are believed to be found nowhere else on the continent. In addition to slough and strand communities, Fakahatchee Strand State Preserve features wet prairies, cypress domes, hardwood hammocks, salt marshes, and mangrove forest. More than ninety-five plant species and forty-two animal species found within the preserve's boundaries are considered to be endangered, threatened, or of special concern. Among these plants are the small catopsis, leafless orchid, ghost orchid, dwarf epidendrum, and auricled spleenwort. Endangered wildlife include the wood stork, Florida panther, Florida black bear, and Big Cypress fox squirrel.

Currently, interpretive facilities and activities within the preserve are limited primarily to the 865-foot approach trail and 2,300-foot boardwalk located at Big Cypress Bend, which is on U.S. 41 approximately seven miles west of State Road 29. The trail/boardwalk system begins at the Indian village and meanders through some of the most magnificent virgin cypress to be found in Big Cypress Swamp. Janes Scenic Drive, which is a few miles north of U.S. 41 on State Road 29, winds through much of the preserve, allowing you either to experience the mosaic of landscapes from your car or to use the road as a starting point for rambles on foot along the many overgrown tramroads that radiate out from the road. These old tramroads are the closest thing you will find to trails leading into the swamp and beautiful backcountry reaches of the preserve. Before taking off on a backcountry hike, the park recommends that you let someone know where you are going and take a compass to avoid getting disoriented, especially if you leave a tramroad and wade into the sloughs. For canoeists, there is a turnoff on the south side of U.S. 41 about one-and-a-half miles east of the Big Cypress Bend that allows you to launch and explore the mangrove wilderness along the East River, which eventually drains into Fakahatchee Bay in the Cape Romano–Ten Thousand Islands Aquatic Preserve.

For more information about Fakahatchee Strand State Preserve, write to Fakahatchee Strand State Preserve, P.O. Box 548, Copeland, FL 33926, or call (941) 695-4593.

CAPE ROMANO–TEN THOUSAND ISLANDS AQUATIC PRESERVE

Cape Romano–Ten Thousand Islands Aquatic Preserve occupies 27,642 acres of the Ten Thousand Islands between Rookery Bay Aquatic Preserve to the west, Collier-Seminole State Park and Fakahatchee Strand State Preserve to the north, and Everglades National Park to the east. Established in October 1969, it was one of the first aquatic preserves and is currently one of forty such preserves in the state system. Florida's Aquatic Preserve program was set up to protect marine, estuarine, and freshwater areas in an essentially natural or existing condition, thereby conserving their aesthetic, biological, and scientific values. Management of the preserve also involves ensuring public recreational opportunities and reviewing and commenting on applications for the use of state-owned submerged lands.

The Cape Romano–Ten Thousand Islands Aquatic Preserve features pristine fringing mangrove forest and mangrove islands, oyster bars, seagrass beds, and other estuarine habitats critical to an extensive array of fish, birds, and other wildlife. Research and environmental education programs are conducted through Rookery Bay National Estuarine Research Reserve in the adjacent Rookery Bay Aquatic Preserve. The Cape Romano–Ten Thousand Islands Aquatic Preserve can be accessed only by water from Marco Island, Collier-Seminole State Park, Port of the Islands (via the FakaUnion Canal), Everglades City, and Chokoloskee. For more information about the aquatic preserve, contact Rookery Bay National Estuarine Research Reserve, 10 Shell Island Road, Naples, FL 33962, or call (941) 775-8845.

The National Audubon Society's Corkscrew Swamp Sanctuary is one of the oldest preserves in Big Cypress Swamp. As early as 1912, an Audubon warden patrolled the Corkscrew Creek (Corkscrew Swamp) region of Big Cypress to prevent plume hunters from shooting great egrets on their nests. At the time, this important area supported some of the largest remaining rookeries of great egrets, wood storks, and other wading birds in southern Florida. However, movement to establish a sanctuary did not occur until 1954, when the Corkscrew Cypress Rookery Association was formed in response to the threat of large-scale cypress logging, drainage, and development. The association, comprised of fourteen separate conservation organizations and many influential individuals, succeeded in working out arrangements to acquire (through outright purchase, donations, and leases) over 6,000 acres of Corkscrew from the Lee Tidewater Cypress Company and the Collier Company, who owned rights to the standing timber. The National Audubon Society accepted responsibility for managing the sanctuary and over time has increased the acreage to 11,000 acres.

Audubon's primary management goal at Corkscrew is preservation of the natural system—a philosophy that allows natural forces to control the ecosystem without favoring certain species over others. The Corkscrew staff implements this philosophy through a program that consists of hydrological monitoring, exotic plant and animal control, prescribed burning, limited human access to the property, and the monitoring of biotic communities. All of the major habitat types of Big Cypress Swamp are found in the sanctuary, including freshwater marshes and wet prairies, cypress swamp, pinelands, and hardwood hammocks.

Public environmental education is another major goal at the sanctuary, and the one-and-three-quarter-mile self-guided trail/boardwalk system (complete with roving interpreters) is the sanctuary's primary educational resource. Points of interest are marked with numbers along the boardwalk and are explained in a guidebook you receive before you begin your walk. The boardwalk winds through a stand of virgin cypress and allows you to witness firsthand the amazing array of plants and wildlife that comprise the cypress swamp system. Exhibits are often set up along the boardwalk to emphasize interesting aspects of cypress swamp ecology or to point out rare sights, such as a swallow-tailed kite nest or a clamshell orchid blooming at the base of a pond apple. A raised platform looks out over the central marsh and provides an excellent view of Corkscrew's wood stork and great egret rookery when the birds gather to mate and raise their young in the spring.

At the eastern edge of the strand, the boardwalk crosses a wet prairie before connecting with the paved trail that meanders through a mature slash pine forest. Deer, quail, marsh rabbits, red-shouldered hawks, and several species of butterflies are common on this area of the trail system. By the time you have finished your tour of Corkscrew Swamp Sanctuary, you will have learned much about the history and ecology of Corkscrew Swamp and Big Cypress Swamp in general.

National Audubon's Corkscrew Swamp Sanctuary is located one-and-a-half miles from County Road 846. The Sanctuary Road entrance (County Road 849) is fourteen miles from Immokalee, twenty-one miles from Route 41, and fifteen miles from I-75, Exit 17. For more information about the sanctuary, contact Corkscrew Swamp Sanctuary, 375 Sanctuary Road, Naples, FL 33964, or call (941) 657-3771.

PLANTS AND WILDLIFE
IN BIG CYPRESS SWAMP AND
THE TEN THOUSAND ISLANDS

TREES AND SHRUBS

Red maple (*Acer rubrum*)
Paurotis palm (*Acoelorrhaphe wrightti*)
Pond apple (*Annona glabra*)
Marlberry (*Ardisia escallonioides*)
Black mangrove (*Avicennia germinans*)
Groundsel tree (*Baccharis halimifolia*)
Bustic (*Bumelia salicifolia*)
Gumbo limbo (*Bursera simaruba*)
Beautyberry (*Callicarpa americana*)
Cocoplum (*Chrysobalanus icaco*)
Satinleaf (*Chrysophyllum oliviforme*)
Pigeon plum (*Coccoloba diversifolia*)
Buttonwood (*Conocarpus erectus*)
Coral bean (*Erythrina herbacea*)
White stopper (*Eugenia axillaris*)
Spanish stopper (*Eugenia foetida*)
Strangler fig (*Ficus aurea*)
Pop ash (*Fraxinus caroliniana*)
Dahoon holly (*Ilex cassine*)
Virginia willow (*Itea virginica*)
White mangrove (*Laguncularia racemosa*)
Primrose willow (*Ludwigia spp.*)
Wild tamarind (*Lysiloma latisiliquum*)
Sweet bay (*Magnolia virginica*)
Mastic (*Mastichodendron foetidissimum*)

Poisonwood (*Metopium toxiferum*)
Simpson's stopper (*Myrcianthes fragrans* var. *simpsonii*)
Wax myrtle (*Myrica cerifera*)
Lancewood (*Ocotea coriacea*)
Red bay (*Persea borbonia*)
Slash pine (*Pinus elliottii*)
Jamaica dogwood (*Piscidia piscipula*)
Wild coffee (*Pyschotria nervosa*)
Laurel oak (*Quercus laurifolia*)
Live oak (*Quercus virginiana*)
Myrsine (*Rapanea punctata*)
Red mangrove (*Rhizophora mangle*)
Royal palm (*Roystonea elata*)
Cabbage palm (*Sabal palmetto*)
Willow (*Salix caroliniana*)
Saw palmetto (*Serenoa repens*)
Pond cypress (*Taxodium ascendens*)
Bald cypress (*Taxodium distichum*)
Wild lime (*Zanthoxylum fagara*)

ORCHIDS

Pine pink (*Bletia purpurea*)
Rat-tail orchid (*Bulbophyllum pachyrhachis*)
Pale grass pink (*Calopogon pallidus*)
Grass pink (*Calopogon tuberosus*)
Crooked-spur orchid (*Campylocentrum pachyrrhizum*)
Cowhorn orchid (*Cyrtopodium punctatum*)
Dollar orchid (*Encyclia boothiana*)
Clamshell orchid (*Encyclia cochleata*)
Dwarf epidendrum (*Encyclia pygmaea*)
Butterfly orchid (*Encyclia tampensis*)
Brown epidendrum (*Epidendrum anceps*)
Ramose orchid (*Epidendrum blancheanum*)
Umbelled epidendrum (*Epidendrum difforme*)
Night orchid (*Epidendrum nocturnum*)
Rigid epidendrum (*Epidendrum rigidum*)

Twisted orchid (*Epidendrum strobiliferum*)
Oak orchid (*Erythrodes querceticola*)
Wild coco (*Eulophia alta*)
False water-spider orchid (*Habenaria distans*)
Snowy orchid (*Habenaria nivea*)
Tooth-petal orchid (*Habenaria odontopetala*)
Long-horned orchid (*Habenaria quinqueseta*)
Water spider orchid (*Habenaria repens*)
Extended orchid (*Harrisella filiformis*)
Delicate orchid (*Ionopsis utricularioides*)
Tiny orchid (*Lepanthopsis melanantha*)
Tall liparis (*Liparis elata*)
Shiny-leaf orchid (*Liparis nervosa*)
Florida malaxis (*Malaxis spicata*)
Maxillaria (*Maxillaria conferta*)
False butterfly orchid (*Maxillaria crassifolia*)
Florida oncidium (*Oncidium floridanum*)
Mule-ear orchid (*Oncidium floridanum*)
Frosted-flower orchid (*Pleurothallis gelida*)
Ghost orchid (*Polyrrhiza lindenii*)
Many-spiked orchid (*Polystacha concreta*)
Shadow witch (*Ponthieva racemosa*)
Nodding ladies' tresses (*Spiranthes cernua* var. *odorata*)
Helmit ladies' tresses (*Spiranthes cranichoides*)
Lace-lip ladies' tresses (*Spiranthes lacinata*)
Red ladies' tresses (*Spiranthes lanceolata* var. *lanceolata*)
Fakahatchee ladies' tresses (*Spiranthes lanceolata* var. *paludicola*)
Long-lip ladies' tresses (*Spiranthes longilabris*)
Giant ladies' tresses (*Spiranthes praecox*)
Spring ladies' tresses (*Spiranthes vernalis*)
Leafy vanilla (*Vanilla phaeantha*)

BROMELIADS

Yellow catopsis (*Catopsis berteroniana*)
Many-flowered catopsis (*Catopsis floribunda*)
Small catopsis (*Catopsis nutans*)

Strap-leaved air plant (*Guzmania monstachia*)
Reflexed wild pine (*Tillandsia balbisiana*)
Twisted air plant (*Tillandsia circinata*)
Stiff-leaved wild pine (*Tillandsia fasciculata*)
Banded wild pine (*Tillandsia flexuosa*)
Reddish wild pine (*Tillandsia polystachia*)
Fuzzy-wuzzy air plant (*Tillandsia pruinosa*)
Ball moss (*Tillandsia recurvatta*)
Needle-leaf air plant (*Tillandsia setacea*)
Spanish moss (*Tillandsia usneoides*)
Giant wild pine (*Tillandsia utriculata*)
Soft-leaved wild pine (*Tillandsia valenzuelana*)

FERNS AND CYCADS

Golden leather fern (*Acrostichum aureum*)
Leather fern (*Acrostichum danaeaefolium*)
Auricled spleenwort (*Asplenium auritum*)
Bird's nest fern (*Asplenium serratum*)
Mosquito fern (*Azolla caroliniana*)
Swamp fern (*Blechnum serrulatum*)
Narrow strap fern (*Campyloneurum angustifolium*)
Narrow strap fern (*Campyloneurum costatum*)
Strap fern (*Campyloneurum phyllitidis*)
Florida tree fern (*Ctenitis sloanei*)
Comb fern (*Ctenitis submarginalis*)
Quillwort (*Isoetes flaccida*)
Club moss (*Lycopodium carolinianum*)
Hanging club moss (*Lycopodium dichotomum*)
Climbing fern (*Microgramma heterophylla*)
Giant sword fern (*Nephrolepis biserrata*)
Sword fern (*Nephrolepis exaltata*)
Hand fern (*Ophioglossum palmatum*)
Adder's tongue fern (*Ophioglossum petiolatum*)
Cinnamon fern (*Osmunda cinnamomea*)
Royal fern (*Osmunda regalis* var. *spectabilis*)
Golden polypody (*Phlebodium aureum*)

Polypody fern (*Polypodium plumula*)
Resurrection fern (*Polypodium polypodioides*)
Polypody fern (*Polypodium ptilodon*)
Whisk fern (*Psiltotum nudum*)
Bracken (*Pteridium aquilinum*)
Ladder brake (*Pteris vittata*)
Water fern (*Salvinia minima*)
Parsley fern (*Sphenomeris clavata*)
Cypress fern (*Thelpyteris reticulata*)
Marsh fern (*Thelypteris interrupta*)
Shoestring fern (*Vittaria lineata*)
Chain fern (*Woodwardia virginica*)
Coontie (*Zamia pumila*)

HERBACEOUS WILDFLOWERS

False foxglove (*Agalinis* spp.)
Aster (*Aster* spp.)
Spanish needles (*Bidens alba*)
Florida bellflower (*Campanula floridana*)
Yellow canna (*Canna flaccida*)
Partridge pea (*Cassia fasciculata*)
Thistle (*Cirsium horridulum*)
Tickseed (*Coreopsis leavenworthii*)
Swamp lily (*Crinum americanum*)
Beggar ticks (*Desmodium paniculatum*)
White-top sedge (*Dichromena colorata*)
White-top sedge (*Dichromena latifolia*)
Southern fleabane (*Erigeron quercifolius*)
Daisy fleabane (*Erigeron strigosus*)
Milk pea (*Galactica* spp.)
Skyflower (*Hydrolea corymbosa*)
Spider lily (*Hymenocallis latifolia*)
Alligator lily (*Hymenocallis palmeri*)
St. John's wort (*Hypericum* spp.)
Yellow-eyed grass (*Hypoxis leptocarpa*)
Moonflower (*Ipomoea alba*)

Morning glory (*Ipomoea cordato-triloba*)
Island morning glory (*Ipomoea indica*)
Iris (*Iris hexagona* var. *savannarum*)
Jacquemontia (*Jacquemontia curtissii*)
Marsh mallow (*Kosteletzkya virginica*)
Blazing star (*Liatris* spp.)
Catesby lily (*Lilium catesbaei*)
Bay lobelia (*Lobelia feayana*)
Glades lobelia (*Lobelia glandulosa*)
Spatterdock (*Nuphar luteum*)
Blue water lily (*Nymphaea elegans*)
White water lily (*Nymphaea odorata*)
Passion flower (*Passiflora incarnata*)
Yellow maypop (*Passiflora lutea*)
Cypress peperomia (*Peperomia glabella*)
Florida peperomia (*Peperomia obtusifolia*)
Red-stemmed peperomia (*Peperomia questeliana*)
Small butterwort (*Pinguicula pumila*)
Marsh fleabane (*Pluchea rosea*)
Pickerelweed (*Pontederia cordata*)
Rubber vine (*Rhabdadenia biflora*)
Black-eyed susan (*Rudbeckia hirta* var. *floridana*)
Wild petunia (*Ruellia caroliniensis*)
Marsh pink (*Sabatia* spp.)
Seaside purslane (*Sesuvium portulacastrum*)
Blue-eyed grass (*Sisyrinchium miamiensis*)
Horned bladderwort (*Utricularia cornuta*)
Floating bladderwort (*Utricularia inflata*)
Blueberry (*Vaccinium corymbosum*)
Ironweed (*Veronia blodgettii*)
Vetch (*Vicia acutifolia*)
Cow pea (*Vigna luteola*)
Rain lily (*Zephyranthes simpsonii*)

Sources for plant lists: Duever (1986) and Austin (n.d.).

BIRDS (NONBREEDING)

Common loon
American widgeon
Northern shoveler
Blue-winged teal
Fulvous whistling duck
Ring-necked duck
Lesser scaup
Red-breasted merganser
Cooper's hawk
Sharp-shinned hawk
Northern harrier
Broad-winged hawk
Peregrine falcon
Merlin
American kestrel
Snail kite
Reddish egret
American bittern
Roseate spoonbill
Virginia rail
Sora
American coot
Black-bellied plover
Piping plover
Semipalmated plover
Whimbrel
Solitary sandpiper
Willet
Greater yellowlegs
Lesser yellowlegs
Short-billed dowitcher
Ruddy turnstone
Red knot
Dunlin
Sanderling

Least sandpiper
Semipalmated sandpiper
Western sandpiper
Common snipe
Herring gull
Ring-billed gull
Forster's tern
Royal tern
Caspian tern
Black tern
Black skimmer
Smooth-billed ani
Whip-poor-will
Belted kingfisher
Yellow-bellied sapsucker
Hairy woodpecker
Eastern phoebe
Tree swallow
Long-billed marsh wren
Short-billed marsh wren
Catbird
American robin
Cedar waxwing
Solitary vireo
Rusty blackbird
Painted bunting
Indigo bunting
Cape May warbler
Black-throated blue warbler
Yellow-rumped warbler
Palm warbler
Blackpoll warbler
Black-and-white warbler
American redstart
Ovenbird

Northern waterthrush
Savannah sparrow
White-throated sparrow
Lincoln's sparrow
Grasshopper sparrow

Henslow's sparrow
Sharp-tailed sparrow
Chipping sparrow
Swamp sparrow

Sources: Duever (1986) and Robertson et al. (1991).

BIRDS (BREEDING)

Pied-billed grebe
Brown pelican
Magnificent frigate bird
Anhinga
Mottled duck
Wood duck
Turkey vulture
Black vulture
Swallow-tailed kite
White-tailed kite
Red-tailed hawk
Red-shouldered hawk
Short-tailed hawk
Southern bald eagle
Osprey
Turkey
Bobwhite
Great egret
Snowy egret
Cattle egret
Great blue heron
Little blue heron
Tricolored heron
Green heron
Black-crowned night heron
Yellow-crowned night heron
Least bittern
Wood stork
Glossy ibis

White ibis
Florida sandhill crane
Limpkin
Black rail
Clapper rail
King rail
Common moorhen
Purple gallinule
Black-necked stilt
Wilson's plover
Killdeer
Laughing gull
Least tern
Common ground dove
Mourning dove
Mangrove cuckoo
Yellow-billed cuckoo
Screech owl
Great horned owl
Barn owl
Barred owl
Chuck-will's widow
Common nighthawk
Ruby-throated hummingbird
Yellow-shafted flicker
Downy woodpecker
Pileated woodpecker
Red-bellied woodpecker
Red-cockaded woodpecker

Eastern kingbird
Gray kingbird
Great crested flycatcher
Purple martin
Blue jay
Common crow
Fish crow
Tufted titmouse
Brown-headed nuthatch
Carolina wren
Northern mockingbird
Brown thrasher
Eastern bluebird
Blue-gray gnatcatcher

Loggerhead shrike
White-eyed vireo
Prothonotary warbler
Northern parula warbler
Common yellowthroat
Pine warbler
Eastern meadowlark
Red-winged blackbird
Common grackle
Boat-tailed grackle
Northern cardinal
Rufous-sided towhee
Bachman's sparrow

Sources: Duever (1986) and Robertson et al. (1991).

REPTILES

American crocodile
American alligator
Florida snapping turtle
Stinkpot turtle
Florida mud turtle
Striped mud turtle
Florida box turtle
Diamondback terrapin
Florida red-bellied turtle
Florida chicken turtle
Gopher tortoise
Florida soft-shelled turtle
Green anole
Six-lined race runner
Ground skink
Southeastern five-lined skink
Eastern glass lizard
Slender glass lizard
Florida green water snake
Florida banded water snake

Brown water snake
Mangrove salt-marsh snake
South Florida swamp snake
Striped crayfish snake
Eastern garter snake
Florida brown snake
South Florida ribbon snake
Eastern hognose snake
Southern ringneck snake
Eastern mud snake
Southern black racer
Everglades racer
Eastern coachwhip
Rough green snake
Eastern indigo snake
Corn snake
Yellow rat snake
Everglades rat snake
Florida king snake
Scarlet king snake

Florida scarlet snake

Florida cottonmouth

Dusky pygmy rattlesnake

Eastern diamondback rattlesnake

Eastern coral snake

Source: Modified from Duever (1986).

AMPHIBIANS

Two-toed amphiuma

Greater siren

Everglades dwarf siren

Peninsula newt

Southern toad

Oak toad

Florida cricket frog

Green tree frog

Barking tree frog

Pine woods tree frog

Squirrel tree frog

Little grass frog

Florida grass frog

Eastern narrow-mouth toad

Southern leopard frog

Pig frog

Source: Duever (1986).

MAMMALS

Opossum

Least shrew

Short-tailed shrew

Eastern yellow bat

Evening bat

Florida black bear

Raccoon

Longtail weasel

Everglades mink

River otter

Spotted skunk

Striped skunk

Gray fox

Florida panther

Bobcat

Eastern gray squirrel

Big Cypress fox squirrel

Cotton mouse

Rice rat

Hispid cotton rat

Florida water rat

Eastern cottontail rabbit

Marsh rabbit

White-tailed deer

Manatee

Bottle-nosed dolphin

Source: Modified from Duever (1986).

BUTTERFLIES

Black swallowtail
Zebra swallowtail
Giant swallowtail
Eastern tiger swallowtail
Spicebush swallowtail
Palamedes swallowtail
Florida white
Checkered white
European cabbage butterfly
Great southern white
Orange sulfur
Large orange sulfur
Cloudless sulfur
Orange barred sulfur
Barred sulfur
Little sulfur
Rambling orange
Dainty sulfur
Coontie atala
Red banded hairstreak
Southern oak hairstreak
White M hairstreak
Gray hairstreak
Bartram's hairstreak
Eastern pygmy blue
Southern blue
Little metalmark
Gulf fritillary
Julia longwing
Zebra longwing
Variegated fritillary
Phaon crescent
Pearl crescent
American painted lady
Red admiral

Buckeye
Black mangrove buckeye
White peacock
Malachite
Viceroy
Florida purplewing
Dingy purplewing
Ruddy daggerwing
Hackberry butterfly
Southern satyr
Georgia satyr
Monarch
Queen
Swarthy skipper
Southern swarthy skipper
Dingy dotted skipper
Clouded skipper
Least skipperling
Tiny skipper
Fiery skipper
Dotted skipper
Gulf coast skipper
Little tawny edge
Whirlabout
Red broken dash
Sachem
Brown rim skipper
Black vein skipper
Golden skipper
Atlantic marsh skipper
Coastal sedge skipper
Palmetto skipper
Sedge witch
Palm skipper
Dusted skipper

Dusky little skipper
Gray skipper
Three spot skipper
Canna skipper
Salt-marsh skipper
Long wing skipper
Mangrove skipper
Silver spotted skipper
Violet skipper
Long-tailed skipper
Brown-tailed skipper

Cloudy wing
Eastern cloudy wing
Dark cloudy wing
Banded oak dusky wing
Eastern oak dusky wing
Brown dusky wing
Streamlined dusky wing
Checkered skipper
Tropical checkered skipper

Source: Gerberg and Arnett (1989).

FISH

The following list includes freshwater and saltwater species found in canals near the coast.
Florida gar
Bowfin
Redfin pickerel
Chain pickerel
Golden shiner
Taillight shiner
Lake chubsucker
Yellow bullhead
Brown bullhead
Sheepshead minnow
Golden topminnow
Marsh killifish
Flagfish
Bluefin killifish
Mosquito fish
Least killifish
Sailfin molly
Brook silverside
Tidewater silverside

Everglades pygmy sunfish
Bluespotted sunfish
Warmouth
Bluegill
Dollar sunfish
Redear sunfish
Spotted sunfish
Largemouth bass
Black crappie
Swamp darter
Striped mojarra
Spotfin mojarra
Tarpon
Snook
Needlefish
Redfin needlefish
Silver jenny
Sheepshead
Striped mullet
Clown goby
Hogchoker
Source: Duever (1986).

COMMON EXOTICS

The exotic (non-native) species identified below are among the most troublesome in Big Cypress Swamp and the Ten Thousand Islands because of their aggressive nature and negative impact on native species.

Plants

Australian pine (*Casuarina* spp.)
Air potato (*Dioscorea bulbifera*)
Water hyacinth (*Eichhornia crassipes*)
Hydrilla (*Hydrilla verticillata*)
Melaleuca (*Melaleuca quinquenervia*)
Brazilian pepper (*Schinus terebinthifolius*)

Reptiles

Cuban (brown) anole

Amphibians

Cuban tree frog
Marine toad

Mammals

Armadillo
Feral hog

Fish

Black acara
Walking catfish

Sources: Duever (1986) and Austin (n.d.).

REFERENCES

Austin, Daniel F. *Vascular Plants of Fakahatchee Strand State Preserve.* Booklet, n.d.

Brook Van Meter, Victoria. *Florida's Alligators and Crocodiles.* Miami: Florida Power and Light Company, 1987.

———. *The Florida Panther.* Miami: Florida Power and Light Company, 1988.

———. *Florida's Wood Stork.* Miami: Florida Power and Light Company, 1985.

———. *The West Indian Manatee in Florida.* Miami: Florida Power and Light Company, 1987.

Davidson, Treat. "Tree Snails, Gems of the Everglades." *National Geographic* 121 (March-April 1964): 372–387.

Deuver, Michael J., et al. *The Big Cypress National Preserve.* New York: National Audubon Society, 1986.

Florida Department of Natural Resources, Division of Parks and Recreation. *A Management Plan for Collier-Seminole State Park.* Tallahassee: Florida Department of Natural Resources, n.d.

———. *A Management Plan for Fakahatchee Strand State Preserve.* Tallahassee: Florida Department of Natural Resources, n.d.

Florida Department of Natural Resources, Division of State Lands, Bureau of Aquatic Preserves. *Rookery Bay and Cape Romano–Ten Thousand Islands Aquatic Preserves Management Plan.* Tallahassee: Florida Department of Natural Resources, 1988.

Gerberg, Eugene J., and Ross H. Arnett, Jr. *Florida Butterflies.* Baltimore: Natural Science Publications, 1989.

Hoffmeister, John Edward. *Land from the Sea: Geologic Story of South Florida.* Coral Gables: University of Miami Press, 1974.

Hooper, Robert G., Andrew F. Robinson, and Jerome A. Jackson. *The Red-Cockaded Woodpecker: Notes on Life History and Management.* Atlanta: U.S. Department of Agriculture, Forest Service, Southeastern Area, State and Private Forestry, 1980.

Kaplan, Eugene H. *Southeastern and Caribbean Seashores.* Peterson Field Guides. Boston: Houghton Mifflin Company, 1988.

Linley, John R. *Biting Midges of Coastal Florida*. Vero Beach: Florida Medical Entomology Laboratory, IFAS–University of Florida, 1990.

Maehr, David S. "Tracking Florida's Panthers." *Defenders* 65, no. 5 (September-October 1990): 10–15.

Myers, Ronald L., and John J. Ewel, eds. *Ecosystems of Florida*. Orlando: University Presses of Florida, 1990.

National Audubon Society. *Management Goals and Objectives at Corkscrew Swamp Sanctuary: A Mission Statement*. Management Report, Corkscrew Swamp Sanctuary, 1984.

Robertson, Jr., William B., et al. *Birds of Everglades National Park*. Florida National Parks and Monuments Association pamphlet. 1991.

Snyder, James R. "Fire Regimes in Subtropical South Florida." In *High Intensity Fire in Wildlands: Management Challenges and Options*. Proceedings, 17th Tall Timbers Fire Ecology Conference, 1991. Tall Timbers Research Station, Tallahassee, Fla.

Stokes, Donald, and Lillian Stokes. *A Guide to Bird Behavior III*. Boston: Little, Brown and Company, 1989.

Tebeau, Charlton W. *Man in the Everglades: 2000 Years of Human History in the Everglades National Park*. Coral Gables: University of Miami Press, 1968.

Toops, Connie. *Everglades*. Stillwater, Minn.: Voyageur Press, 1989.

U.S. Department of the Interior, Fish and Wildlife Service. *A Draft Management Summary and Objectives for Florida Panther National Wildlife Refuge*. Naples: Florida Panther National Wildlife Refuge, 1991.

U.S. Department of the Interior, National Park Service. Big Cypress National Preserve. *Draft General Management Plan and Draft Environmental Impact Statement*. Denver: U.S. Government Printing Office, 1989.

U.S. Department of the Interior, National Park Service. Everglades National Park. *Gulf Coast Everglades National Park Draft Development Concept Plan and Environmental Assessment*. Denver: Government Printing Office, 1990.